Reiki and Shadow Work: Healing the Dark Side of the Soul

Copy Editor and Interior Design: Constance Santego
Book Layout: ©2017 BookDesignTemplates.com

Ordering Information:
Quantity sales. Special discounts are available on quantity purchases by corporations, associations, and others. For details, contact the address below.

Trade paperback ISBN: 978-1-997907-16-9

eBook ISBN 978-1-997907-17-6

Created and published In Canada. Printed and bound in the United States of America

First Edition
Published by Maximillian Enterprises
Kelowna, BC Canada
www.constancesantego.ca

Reiki and Shadow Work: Healing the Dark Side of the Soul

REIKI WISDOM SERIES

Beyond the Symbols — The Path to True Mastery

Sacred Symbol of Reiki Wisdom

The sacred combination of the **circle**, **triangle**, **intersecting lines**, and **pentagram** represents the harmonious flow of spiritual and physical energy.

- The **circle** symbolizes **wholeness** and **spiritual protection**, reflecting the infinite and interconnected nature of Reiki energy.
- The **triangle** embodies **creation** and **balance**, representing the three pillars of Reiki — **mind**, **body**, and **spirit** — working in harmony.
- The **three converging lines** reflect **unity** and **focused intent**, directing energy flow through the chakras and meridians.
- The **pentagram** signifies **mastery of the elements** (earth, fire, water, air, and spirit) and the awakening of spiritual wisdom.

This symbol represents the manifestation of divine energy into physical reality through balance, alignment, and focused intention. It reflects the path to enlightenment — where mind, body, and spirit align to unlock deep healing and spiritual mastery.

Grand Master, Constance Santego

REIKI AND SHADOW WORK: HEALING THE DARK SIDE OF THE SOUL

VOL. IV OF THE REIKI WISDOM SERIES

Beyond the Symbols — The Path to True Mastery

Dr. Constance Santego

Maximillian Enterprises
Kelowna, BC

Dedication

To those who have faced their darkness and
chosen to heal,
To the brave souls who sit with their pain
instead of running from it,
And to the seekers who know that wholeness
lies not in perfection, but in integration—
This book is for you.

May it be your lantern in the shadows,
your sanctuary in the storm,
and your invitation to reclaim every part of
who you are.

"True healing begins when you face the parts of yourself you were taught to hide.
With Reiki, you don't just illuminate the shadow—you transform it into light."

—Dr. Constance Santego

ALSO BY DR. CONSTANCE SANTEGO

NOVELS

Illegitimate Grace
Ashcroft Hollow

Okanagan Trilogy:
Beneath the Vineyards
Under the Okanagan Sun
Guardian of the Lake

The Nine Spiritual Gifts Series:
Journey of a Soul – (Vol 1 Michael)
Language of a Soul – (Vol 2 Gabriel)
Prophecy of a Soul – (Vol 3 Bath Kol)
Healing of a Soul – (Vol 4 Raphael)
Miracles of a Soul – (Vol 5 Hamied)
Knowledge of a Soul – (Vol 6 Raziel)
Wisdom of a Soul – (Vol 7 Uriel)
Faith of a Soul – (Vol 8 Pistis Sophia)

NONFICTION

The Intuitive Life, The Gift Of Prophecy, Third Edition
Fairy Tales, Dreams And Reality… *Where Are You On Your Path? Second Edition*
Your Persona… The Mask You Wear
Archangel Michael's Soul Retrieval Guide
Bend, Don't Break: *Finding Your Way Back To Abundance*
Ring Therapy: *A Guide To Healing And Balance*
Ring Therapy Pocket Guide
Beyond The Mind: *Harnessing The Power Of Astral Projection For Creative Awakening*
Floraopathy™: *The Art And Science Of Vibrational Healing With Essential Oils*
Dear Older Me: A Memoir… *Of Sorts*
It's Just Like Poker: *A Spiritual Guide To Playing The Cards Life Deals You*
Signs And Meanings: *What The Feet Reveal About Health, Stress, And The Body's Story*
Auricions: *Unlocking Subconscious Healing Through Quantum Medicine*

Quick Fix Acupressure Method
Manifestation – *The DREAM Method in 5 Steps*
Confidence – *Mastering the Dream Method*
The New Paradigm: Conscious Healing In The Age Of Ai
Shadow & Light: A Guide to Healing the Hidden Self

TESLA SERIES:
Tesla And The Future Of Energy Medicine
Beyond Tesla: *Advancing The Science Of Energy Healing*
Tesla's Code: *Mastering Energy, Frequency, And Creative Power*
Tesla's Bioenergetic Blueprint: *Healing the Human Field Through Frequency, Mapping & Coherence*

REIKI WISDOM, SERIES:
Angelic Lifestyle, a Vibrant Lifestyle
Angelic Lifestyle 42-Day Energy Cleanse
Reiki and the Power of The Joint Points: Unlocking Energy Pathways for Healing (Vol I)
Reiki and Karmic Healing: Releasing Patterns From Past Lives (Vol II)
Reiki and the Five Elements (Vol III)
Secrets of a Healer, Magic Of Reiki
The Reiki Master's Manual *(In English, German, Spanish, French, Portuguese, Russian, Hindi, and Mandarin Chinese)*

CHAKRA SERIES:
Heart Chakra 101: The Bridge
Root Chakra 101: Building Safety, Survival, Foundation
Sacral Chakra 101: Creativity, Pleasure, Emotions
Solar Plexus Chakra 101: Power, Confidence, Will
Throat Chakra 101: Truth, Voice, Self-Expression
Third Eye Chakra 101: Intuition, Vision, Insight
Crown Chakra 101: Spiritual Connection, Transcendence.

SECRETS OF A HEALER, SERIES:
Magic Of Aromatherapy (Vol I)
Magic Of Reflexology (Vol II)
Magic Of The Gifts (Vol III)
Magic Of Muscle Testing (Vol IV)
Magic Of Iridology (Vol V)
Magic Of Massage (Vol VI)

Magic Of Hypnotherapy (Vol VII)
Magic Of Reiki (Vol VIII)
Magic Of Advanced Aromatherapy (Vol IX)
Magic Of Esthetics (Vol X)
The Reiki Master's Manual (Vol XI)

ADULT COLORING JOURNALS
SERIES-ZEN COLORING:
Quantum Energy and Mindful Living Journal (Vol 1)
Reiki Energy Journal (Vol 2)
Nine Spiritual Gifts Journal (Vol 3)
I Forgive Journal (Vol 4)

FOR CHILDREN
I am Big Tonight. I Don't Need the Light
The Magic Elf Book: 25 Days of Surprises

COOKBOOK
My Favorite Recipes, with a Hint of Giggle

BUISNESS
How To Use ChatGPT For Authors: From Idea To Published Book
Scaling Beyond 6 Figures: Strategies For Health & Wellness Professionals
The Academypreneur's Playbook: Turn Knowledge Into A Revenue-Generating School

HUMOR/GIFT BOOK
How Do You Like Your Eggs? *Crack Into Your Personality, Yolk and All*

Contents

Preface

Shadow work is not a new concept. It is as ancient as humanity itself. Long before it was named in psychological language, healers, shamans, and spiritual teachers understood that the human soul holds both light and memory — both potential and wounding. They knew that the path to freedom required courage, presence, and sacred compassion for the parts of ourselves we rarely show to the world.

Reiki, too, has its origin in a simple but profound truth: we are more than the physical body. We are vibration, consciousness, and living energy. When we interact with this energy intentionally, change occurs in places deeper than thought — in the subtle architecture of the mind, emotions, and soul.

This book is born from the meeting of those two truths.

Many approach Reiki as a method of comfort, relaxation, and gentle release. And it is all of those things. But Reiki can also be a catalyst — a light that reveals the inner terrain we have carried for years. When used with wisdom, it illuminates what has remained unspoken, unseen, or misunderstood within us. It makes the unconscious visible, not to expose our wounds, but to free them.

Shadow work often has a reputation of being heavy or frightening. In truth, the shadow is not the darkness itself —

it is the light that has been blocked. It is the emotional weight we never had words for. It is the pain that once felt too overwhelming to face. When approached without support, the journey inward can feel isolating. But with Reiki as a gentle guide, the descent into the self becomes balanced, compassionate, and profoundly healing.

Reiki does not force revelation. It does not demand anything from the shadow. Instead, it creates a field of safety and alignment — a space where we can meet our hidden beliefs, stored emotions, and protective behaviors without judgment. In that space, transformation becomes possible.

Over the years, I have witnessed countless students, clients, and practitioners bravely step into their own inner darkness. I have seen their stories unravel, their burdens lift, and their hearts open wider than they ever imagined. Not because the shadow was conquered, but because it was finally met — with truth, tenderness, and energetic support.

This work is deeply personal, but it is also universal. There is no human being who moves through life without carrying imprints from their past — emotional patterns, inherited beliefs, or unprocessed grief. The shadow is part of our shared humanity. To heal it is to reclaim our most authentic expression of self.

In these pages, you will find practices, meditations, reflections, and energy-based approaches to shadow inquiry. But above all, you will find an invitation: to witness yourself honestly, gently, and whole-heartedly. Reiki is the light you will carry with you as you go.

Take your time with this book. Move slowly, breathe deeply, and honor whatever arises. Shadow work is not a race, nor is it a destination. It is a continual unfolding — a relationship with the deepest parts of your inner world.

Whether you are a seasoned healer, a curious student, or someone quietly seeking emotional liberation, may this work bring clarity to your inner landscape, relief to your heart, and a renewed sense of sovereignty over your life.

May your journey through the shadow reveal the truth that has always lived beneath it:

You are whole.
You are worthy.
And even in the darkness, you are never without light.

Dr. Constance Santego
Grand Reiki Master

Note to Reader

A Word on Shadow Work, Responsibility, and the Power of Reiki

This work is sacred, emotional, and transformative.
Move slowly, breathe deeply, and be gentle with yourself.

Reiki is a subtle yet powerful form of energy healing—one that moves through the physical, emotional, mental, and spiritual layers of your being. When paired with shadow work, it becomes a compassionate guide into the places within us that have gone unspoken: the wounds we've buried, the stories we've inherited, and the parts of ourselves we learned to hide.

This book is an invitation into deep personal transformation, but it is not a substitute for therapy, counseling, or medical care. If you are navigating trauma, mental health concerns, or physical illness, please seek the support of qualified professionals. Reiki complements professional pathways—it does not replace them.

Shadow work takes us into the roots: early conditioning, unprocessed emotion, limiting beliefs, and often, unconscious fear. Reiki helps soften the edges, regulate the nervous system, and create energetic safety as you explore your inner world. But this journey requires responsibility. Healing is not something that happens "to" you. It is something you engage with, choose, and allow—moment by moment.

At times, the material that surfaces may feel intense. If emotions rise, know that this is not a sign to abandon the work—it is a sign to pause, ground, and return with presence.

Take rest. Journal. Sit with your breath. Receive Reiki. Reach out for support if needed.
Healing is not linear. It is a spiral—each layer revealing more truth, more clarity, and more love.

In these pages, you will explore:

- The foundational principles of shadow work
- Reiki-based techniques to navigate emotional triggers
- Practices for resolving inner conflict and self-sabotage
- Chakra-focused energy balancing
- Journaling prompts, rituals, and meditations
- Tools for reintegration, empowerment, and spiritual remembrance

Integration takes time. Allow space between insights. Let the body process, the mind unwind, and the heart open. Some realizations are immediate. Others require silence, rest, or stillness before they soften into wisdom.

Important Practitioner Guidelines:

- A Level II Reiki certificate is required to offer paid Reiki sessions to others.
- A Level III (Master/Teacher) certificate is required to teach Reiki or provide attunements.

Whether you are a practitioner or a seeker, know that this book meets you in your wholeness—not only in your strength, clarity, and compassion, but also in your uncertainty, pain, and vulnerability.

You are not broken.
You are becoming aware.
And awareness is the first step toward freedom.

Reiki does not fix you.
It reminds you—
of your strength,
your worth,
and your truth.

With compassion and courage,
Dr. Constance Santego
Grand Reiki Master

Learning Outcome

Reiki and Shadow Work: Healing the Dark Side of the Soul

This book is a transformative guide that unites the emotional depth of shadow work with the spiritual intelligence of Reiki healing. It provides a grounded, compassionate path for navigating emotional wounds, unconscious patterns, inner conflict, and the parts of yourself that were once suppressed, rejected, or misunderstood.

Drawing from psychological insight, energetic medicine, and practices of spiritual integration, this work goes beyond surface-level self-help and into the true terrain of inner alchemy. Through practical tools, Reiki techniques, journaling, and ritual, you will learn to meet your shadow not as an enemy to fix — but as a forgotten fragment of yourself to reclaim, honor, and integrate.

Whether you are new to energy medicine or an experienced Reiki practitioner, this book will empower you to use Reiki as a tool for emotional release, spiritual remembrance, nervous system regulation, and deep self-acceptance. By the final chapter, you will have the understanding and skill to begin — or deepen — your own inner healing, and to support others with integrity, presence, and energetic sensitivity.

By the end of this book, you will have gained a comprehensive understanding of:

Part 1: The Psychology and Energy of the Shadow

• What the shadow self is, and how it forms through conditioning, repression, trauma, ancestral memory, and survival patterns
• How unconscious beliefs, emotional triggers, and unprocessed memories influence behavior, relationships, and energetic alignment
• The connection between shadow traits, auric distortions, and blocked chakras
• Reiki as a safe, non-judgmental method for emotional inquiry, energetic release, and compassionate inner dialogue
• The role of the nervous system in shadow healing (fight, flight, freeze, fawn) and how Reiki supports regulation and safety
• The difference between genuine healing and spiritual bypassing — and how to ensure your work remains rooted, embodied, and authentic

Part 2: Reiki Techniques for Emotional Integration

• Chakra-based approaches for addressing emotional wounds, psychological fragmentation, and inner-child imprints
• Using Reiki to soften emotional resistance, calm triggers, and create inner stability during difficult realizations
• Reiki meditations and visualizations for meeting wounded parts of self with compassion, honesty, and light
• How to use hand placements, symbols, emotional extraction intention, and breathwork to hold space for the shadow
• Creating safe, energetic containers for personal processing, reflection, and release
• The Reiki Mirror Work Ritual for self-acceptance, emotional truth, and inner reconciliation

Part 3: Working with Triggers, Trauma, and Inner Conflict

• How to identify the emotional root of triggers and understand what they reveal about the subconscious self
• The energetic roots of self-sabotage, shame, guilt, feelings of unworthiness, and patterns of emotional survival — and how to transmute them
• Techniques for dialoguing with the inner critic, befriending the shadow archetypes, and healing the wounded inner child
• The use of journaling, body awareness, and Reiki attunement to track, discharge, and re-pattern stored emotional energy
• Case examples and session frameworks illustrating shadow integration through Reiki practice
• How to work gently with emotional activation without retraumatization by using grounding, breath, and compassionate pacing

Part 4: Integration, Wholeness, and Spiritual Empowerment

• How to move from fragmentation into integration using Reiki, emotional presence, intentional visualization, auric regulation, and conscious awareness
• Energetic rituals for releasing shame, dissolving emotional residue, and reclaiming lost or suppressed aspects of personal power
• Understanding the symbolic and spiritual purpose of the "dark night of the soul" as a passageway into higher consciousness
• How to connect with your Higher Self, spiritual guides, and inner wisdom to anchor compassion, maturity, and self-trust
• Maintaining energetic boundaries, emotional hygiene, and self-care when working with shadow material — for yourself and others
• Developing your own shadow-healing toolkit using Reiki, breath, contemplation, body grounding, journaling, and emotional reflection

A Journey of Inner Alchemy

This book is both a roadmap and a mirror.

It offers step-by-step methods for engaging with the hidden parts of your psyche — and also invites you to see your wholeness through new eyes. Whether you are supporting your own healing or guiding the healing of others, you will gain the energetic insight, emotional intelligence, and practical skills needed to move from fear into freedom, from contraction into clarity, and from fragmentation into profound inner unity.

Shadow work is not about erasing the darkness.
It is about illuminating it with love.

Reiki is the light that leads you home.

Introduction – Turning Toward the Shadow with Reiki

In traditional Reiki teachings, we learn to work with universal life force energy to bring balance to the body, mind, and spirit. We're taught to place hands over chakras, clear the aura, and allow energy to flow where it's most needed. These principles form the foundation of a beautiful healing art—but there is a deeper layer of Reiki that quietly calls to those ready to listen.

Over the years, in my own practice and in guiding thousands of students and clients, I've noticed a common theme: no matter how skilled we become, some wounds resist healing. They return as emotional triggers, recurring fears, sabotaging behaviors, or quiet self-doubt. They surface in relationships, career blocks, health issues, or moments when we feel lost or fragmented.

These are not always wounds from the outer world.
They are echoes from the inner one—the parts of ourselves we have denied, buried, or labeled as "too much," "not enough," or "unlovable." This is the domain of the **shadow.**

Shadow work invites us to turn inward—not to fight or fix ourselves, but to *see* ourselves fully. It is the path of wholeness, where healing occurs not by escaping pain, but by meeting it with compassion. When paired with Reiki, shadow work becomes not only possible, but sacred. Reiki offers the safety, spaciousness, and energetic support needed to face what once felt unbearable.

This book is your guide for walking that path.

You'll explore how to:

- Recognize emotional triggers and unravel their deeper meaning
- Use Reiki to calm and balance the nervous system while doing deep emotional work
- Work with chakras as emotional memory centers, especially for shame, guilt, and fear
- Apply hand placements, breath, and visualization to integrate rejected inner parts
- Use guided journaling, ritual, and energy tools to safely embrace your shadow
- Develop the discernment to know when to pause, when to process, and when to release

You'll also learn how to apply Reiki-based techniques to dissolve patterns like self-sabotage, perfectionism, or codependency—not as flaws, but as protective strategies your shadow created for survival.

Through each chapter, we'll return again and again to the truth that **healing is not about becoming better. It's about becoming whole.**

This is not light work—but it is sacred work. It is for the soul ready to reclaim its power, its truth, and its presence in the world—not just the polished parts, but the raw, messy, beautiful whole.

Whether you are brand new to Reiki or a seasoned Master, this book is your invitation to expand your healing practice beyond light into integration. The shadow is not your enemy. It is your teacher. And Reiki is the light that allows you to sit beside it, listen, and love it home.

Let this book be your companion through the dark—not to chase the darkness away,
but to bring your light into it.

With reverence for the path and the soul who walks it,
Dr. Constance Santego
Grand Reiki Master

Chapter 1:
Understanding
Shadow Work
and Reiki

Chapter 1: Understanding Shadow Work and Reiki

Where Psychology Meets Energy Healing

Before we can explore how Reiki supports shadow integration, we must first understand what "the shadow" actually is, how the concept emerged, and why it has always been a central pillar of human transformation — long before modern language or therapeutic frameworks existed.

Shadow work is not a trend. It is not a spiritual challenge or a psychological experiment. It is one of the oldest pathways of healing known to the human soul: the inward journey to recover the aspects of oneself that have been forgotten, buried, rejected, or exiled.

Whether expressed through ritual, ceremony, mythology, religion, psychology, energy medicine, or mysticism, every culture has recognized the same core truth:

The parts of ourselves that we avoid are the very parts that shape our lives the most.

Reiki gives us the energetic safety to explore this truth — gently, honestly, and without self-harm. But to appreciate that relationship, we begin with the origins of shadow work and the evolution of its understanding.

THE PSYCHOLOGICAL ORIGINS OF SHADOW WORK

Carl Jung and the Unconscious Self

The word "shadow" entered mainstream awareness primarily through the work of Swiss psychoanalyst Carl Gustav Jung (1875–1961). While Sigmund Freud focused on repressed desires, Jung explored the depths of the psyche — including dreams, symbolism, archetypes, mythology, spirituality, and the unconscious.

Jung described the shadow as:

"The unknown dark side of the personality... everything the subject refuses to acknowledge about himself and yet is always thrusting itself upon him."

In Jung's view, the shadow forms from the traits, impulses, emotions, and memories we pushed aside because they felt unsafe, unacceptable, shameful, or painful. Over time, those hidden fragments became energetically charged and psychologically influential.

Examples include:

- emotions that were not welcome in childhood
- instincts that conflicted with family or cultural expectations
- unmet needs that became coping behaviors
- feelings suppressed for personal survival

Rather than disappearing, these unresolved parts live in our subconscious and emotional body. Without awareness, we act through them — projecting anger, repeating sabotage patterns, or recreating familiar emotional climates.

Jung believed that the goal of psychological wholeness was **integration** — bringing awareness to the shadow so we could reclaim authenticity, personal responsibility, and inner harmony.

In this sense, shadow work is not about excavating darkness. It is about **reuniting with what was separated inside us**.

THE ANCIENT ROOTS OF SHADOW WORK

Shamanic Traditions, Ritual Descent, and Soul Retrieval

Long before Jung, shadow work existed within ancient cultural traditions — though under different names.

Many indigenous and spiritual systems taught forms of:

- soul retrieval
- dream medicine
- ancestor healing
- emotional extraction
- karmic unraveling
- purification rites
- initiatory darkness

In shamanic practice, emotional wounding or inner fragmentation was seen as a form of **soul loss** — where parts of one's essence withdrew or hid due to trauma, fear, shock, grief, abandonment, or shame.

Healers would guide individuals into altered states, symbolic journeys, or energetic realms to retrieve the missing fragments of the self.

These rituals taught that:

- no part of the soul is evil
- every wound holds wisdom
- pain stores power
- the path to healing requires courage and compassion

In many traditions, healing was not imposed externally; it arose from reconnection with one's essence. In this way, shamanic descent mythology mirrors modern shadow integration:

The individual must descend into the inner night to recover what was left behind.

Reiki reflects this same principle — not through force, but through gentle presence, attunement, and conscious energy flow.

INNER CHILD WORK AND EMOTIONAL MEMORY

Where Psychology Meets Soul Healing

Another foundation of shadow work emerges through **inner child work**, which recognizes that a large portion of our emotional and energetic imprints are formed in childhood.

Children are sensitive, open, intuitive, and deeply emotional. They absorb:

- beliefs
- tone of voice
- unspoken tensions
- energetic dynamics
- family conditioning
- relational wounds

When a child experiences shame, neglect, fear, rejection, lack of safety, or emotional abandonment — even accidentally — they adapt.

They learn to hide:

- their truth
- their needs
- their voice
- their softness
- their vulnerabilities
- their emotional authenticity

These adaptations become the adult shadow.

Inner child work acknowledges:

- the nervous system remembers
- the body stores emotion
- the psyche preserves what it cannot express
- the soul contracts around pain to survive

Reiki supports this rediscovery process by holding the emotional body in unconditional compassion, soothing fear responses, and gently loosening the energetic tightness around wounded memories.

WHY THE SHADOW EXISTS

Protection, Not Punishment

Whether viewed through psychological, spiritual, or energetic lenses, the shadow forms for one reason:

Self-protection.

When a child, or even an adult, experiences overwhelming emotion, the psyche safeguards itself by hiding what feels unsafe.

The shadow becomes:

- a vault
- a shield
- a container for wound-memory

Many of these patterns remain unconscious because they served a purpose at some point in our lives.

Shadow work, therefore, is not self-attack.
It is self-understanding.

Instead of ripping open the vault, we unlock it with patience and compassion.

Reiki, with its softness and intelligence, is perfectly suited for this.

How Reiki Complements Shadow Work

Energetic Illumination and Safety

Reiki is universal life force energy — gentle, intelligent, and deeply supportive. When applied to shadow work, Reiki creates:

✓ calm within emotional activation
✓ softness around painful memories
✓ energetic safety for exploration
✓ compassion toward wounded aspects
✓ harmony between the conscious and subconscious

Reiki does not force the shadow to emerge.
Instead, it allows layers to rise naturally, at the pace that feels safe.

Under Reiki, emotions release more smoothly, tension loosens, and clarity emerges. The nervous system softens, allowing the psyche to reveal what has long been hidden.

Shadow material that might otherwise feel overwhelming becomes approachable.

Grief becomes a doorway.
Fear becomes information.
Anger becomes a message.
Shame becomes a point of reconnection.

The shadow begins to feel less like a monster in the dark and more like a child locked in a room — waiting to be acknowledged, comforted, and welcomed home.

WHOLENESS AS THE GOAL

The purpose of shadow work is not perfection, purity, or emotional control.
It is reclamation.

It is remembering that we are far larger, wiser, and more multidimensional than the identities we created to survive.

Reiki and shadow work together guide us toward:

- emotional honesty
- nervous system healing
- chakra realignment
- karmic resolution
- inner-child reconciliation
- expanded intuition
- spiritual maturity
- compassionate self-awareness

This chapter lays the foundation for everything that follows.

Here, we recognize:

- where the shadow originated
- why it formed
- and how Reiki becomes the light we carry into the inner night

As you move deeper into this work, you will begin to see that healing the shadow is not an act of fixing the self — it is the return to wholeness.

And the journey has only just begun.

PRINCIPLES OF REIKI ENERGY AND SPIRITUAL ALIGNMENT

Reiki as the Light That Guides the Descent

To understand how Reiki supports shadow work, it is important to remember what Reiki truly is. Reiki is not force, manipulation, willpower, or emotional bypass. It is a sacred intelligence — a field of universal life energy that flows in harmony with the soul's highest good.

Reiki reveals, but does not overwhelm.
It heals, but does not invade.
It illuminates, but does not accuse.

These principles are the foundation that make Reiki an ideal companion for shadow integration.

1. Universal Life Force Energy

At its essence, Reiki is the current of intelligent energy that animates all living things. It flows naturally through the subtle body, chakras, meridians, and auric field, restoring balance where there is distortion or stagnation.

When used in shadow work, Reiki:

- softens inner resistance
- heightens emotional awareness
- loosens energetic contractions around past wounds
- reveals what has been hidden without forcing revelation

Rather than demanding change, Reiki quietly encourages release, reorganization, and reconnection.

It supports the nervous system, dissolves emotional heaviness, and allows memories to surface at the pace the inner self feels safe.

2. Harmony, Not Opposition

One of the most crucial principles in shadow healing is that Reiki never works against the shadow.

It does not attempt to silence emotions, bury memories, or "correct" personality traits. Instead, it creates inner alignment by allowing the conscious and unconscious self to meet one another with compassion.

When Reiki flows through the emotional body, it communicates:

"What you feel matters. What you remember is valid. What you fear is human. And all of it deserves love."

This changes the energetic tone of the inner landscape. The shadow, long accustomed to being rejected, begins to soften — because it is finally being listened to rather than suppressed.

3. Non-Attachment and Non-Judgment

Reiki energy holds no judgment, blame, guilt, or agenda. This is vital in shadow work, where the most common emotional block is shame.

Many people resist shadow healing because they fear:

- what they might discover
- what they might have to admit
- who they might "really be"

But Reiki approaches every wound, memory, and belief with neutrality.

It reminds us that:

- emotion is information
- behavior is adaptation
- pain is protection
- and the shadow is evidence of survival

When the inner self meets Reiki, shame begins to dissolve.
Where shame relaxes, honesty becomes possible.
And where honesty is present, integration begins.

4. Trust in Inner Wisdom

Reiki operates with its own intelligence.
It flows where it is needed and stops where it is not welcome.

This makes it a powerful ally in shadow work, because it honors:

- personal readiness
- emotional thresholds
- nervous system tolerance

If the psyche is not yet ready to face a memory, emotion, or realization, Reiki will not force the door open. It supports healing with the precision and compassion that only intuitive energy can provide.

Shadow healing requires this respect.
Forcing the inner self to reveal trauma before it is ready can retraumatize rather than resolve.

Reiki never pushes — it invites.

5. Alignment of Body, Mind, and Spirit

Shadow material is not only psychological — it lives in:

- muscle tension
- breathing patterns
- nervous system responses
- energy field contractions
- chakra imbalances
- habitual emotional chemistry

Because Reiki works through all layers of being, it restores coherence between:

- the story we tell ourselves
- the emotions we feel
- the behaviors we repeat
- the energy we emit
- the wounds we still carry

When all levels align, insight deepens, compassion expands, and healing no longer feels like a battle — it becomes reconciliation.

6. Reiki as a Channel of Higher Consciousness

Reiki is an attunement-based lineage practice. When one is attuned, they become a conduit for divine energy — the same intelligence that flows through creation, consciousness, and spiritual remembrance.

During shadow healing, this channel helps:

- illuminate misbeliefs
- reveal hidden pain
- soften emotional edges

- reawaken inner truth
- reconnect the fragmented self to spiritual identity

Where trauma disconnects, Reiki reconnects.
Where fear contracts, Reiki restores flow.
Where shame silences, Reiki reopens the voice.

It supports the return to spiritual coherence — the memory of wholeness that existed before emotional patterns were formed.

7. Integration Over Purification

Shadow work with Reiki is not about "purging negativity." Nothing within you is disposable.

Reiki teaches that every piece of the psyche — even the uncomfortable parts — was born from a need for protection, belonging, or love.

Integration is the goal:

- not erasing
- not cleansing
- not overpowering

The shadow is not a contaminant.
It is energy waiting to be transmuted into wisdom.

Reiki supports that transformation by helping you:

- be present
- feel safe
- stay grounded
- remain compassionate
- and listen deeply

As emotional knots loosen, shadow traits evolve into gifts:

- sensitivity becomes empathy
- self-protection becomes discernment
- anger becomes boundary
- vulnerability becomes honesty
- shame becomes humility
- fear becomes intuition

Reiki alchemizes what once felt heavy into something sacred.

8. The Principle of Oneness

Reiki recognizes that all aspects of the self — conscious and unconscious, light and shadow — are expressions of the same divine source. Nothing within you is separate, wrong, or unworthy.

Shadow work, in this light, becomes less about fixing and more about remembering:

You are already whole.
You are already enough.
You are already connected to Source.

Reiki simply helps you rediscover the parts of yourself that forgot.

REIKI AND THE RETURN TO WHOLENESS

When we apply Reiki to the psyche, we do not attack the shadow — we listen to it.
We give it voice, space, and compassion.
We release the energetic weight around old stories.
We reclaim what was once hidden from view.

The shadow becomes a doorway.
Reiki becomes the light that leads us through it.

Together, they form a path of spiritual maturity, emotional truth, and deep inner alignment — one that honors your past, awakens your present, and liberates your future.

The journey is not about becoming a new self.
It is about becoming a true self.

And with Reiki as your guide, every step inward becomes a step toward home.

How Shadow Work and Reiki Complement Each Other

Two Paths, One Purpose: Wholeness

Shadow work and Reiki may seem like separate disciplines at first glance — one rooted in psychology and emotional excavation, the other in spiritual healing through universal life energy. Yet when placed side by side, they become two sides of the same transformational path.

Where shadow work reveals, Reiki restores.
Where the psyche speaks its truth, Reiki holds that truth in compassion.
Where emotional fragmentation rises to the surface, Reiki weaves coherence back into the subtle body.

Together, they form a complete framework for inner healing.

1. Shadow Work Brings Awareness — Reiki Brings Safety

Shadow work asks us to look honestly at:

- old wounds
- unconscious beliefs
- protective behaviors
- lingering emotional memory

But awareness alone can be confronting. Facing grief, anger, or shame without grounding can overwhelm the nervous system, triggering resistance or shutdown.

Reiki acts as the energetic buffer.

It brings safety to the parts of us that feel exposed, softened presence to the emotions that feel raw, and a stabilizing frequency to the memories that rise during deep introspection.

Shadow work opens the door.
Reiki makes it safe to walk through.

2. Shadow Work Reveals Patterns — Reiki Releases the Charge

Shadow work shows us *why* we behave, think, feel, or react the way we do. It exposes the origin of emotional imprints and survival patterns.

Reiki gently dissolves the energetic residue around those patterns, helping to:

- release stored emotion
- loosen trauma imprints
- rewire conditioned responses
- restore energetic flow to blocked chakras

Shadow work brings the truth to light.
Reiki helps the body, mind, and energy field let go.

3. Shadow Work Works with the Mind — Reiki Works with the Energy

Shadow inquiry involves:

- reflection
- emotional awareness
- psychological honesty
- introspection
- journaling
- witnessing the subconscious

Reiki bypasses the analytical mind, reaching deeper into:

- the auric field
- the chakras
- the nervous system
- memory imprints
- emotional vibration
- karmic echoes

When these layers move together, healing becomes multi-dimensional.

The mind understands.
The spirit relaxes.
The body releases.
The energy reorganizes.

It is integration, not just awareness.

4. Shadow Work Helps Us Meet the Wound — Reiki Helps Us Embrace It

Many people avoid shadow work because they expect pain, judgment, or self-rejection. They fear that what lives inside them is "too much" or "too dark."

Reiki neutralizes that fear.

Its energetic field carries unconditional love. When the shadow emerges within the presence of Reiki, it is met with:

- compassion
- softness
- curiosity
- acceptance

Instead of resisting the pain, we learn to sit with it.

Instead of blaming the inner child or wounded self, we see those fragments as protectors and survivors.

Shadow work gives voice to the inner wound.
Reiki gives it permission to heal.

5. Shadow Work Uncovers the Archetypes — Reiki Transforms Them

Within the shadow live potent psychological archetypes:

- the Inner Critic
- the Saboteur
- the Protector
- the Wounded Child
- the Abandoned One
- the Martyr
- the Mask

Shadow work teaches us to identify and understand these archetypal forms as expressions of emotional memory.

Reiki supports their transformation by:

- releasing shame
- dissolving fear
- calming inner conflict
- balancing the chakras tied to those archetypes
- integrating those parts back into a unified sense of Self

Through Reiki, the archetypes evolve:

- the Critic becomes discernment
- the Saboteur becomes intuition

- the Wounded Child becomes wisdom
- the Protector becomes boundaries

What once felt heavy becomes a source of inner mastery.

6. Shadow Work Confronts Truth — Reiki Anchors Compassion

Shadow work requires honesty.
Sometimes the truths we uncover are uncomfortable.

Reiki ensures that those truths are held within compassion instead of self-condemnation.

It reminds us that:

- past behaviors were survival strategies
- emotional reactions were protective reflexes
- limiting beliefs were once forms of safety

Where the shadow reveals the wound, Reiki whispers:

"You did what you could with what you knew. And now you are ready to heal."

This energetic compassion prevents shame from reattaching to the shadow as it rises.

7. Shadow Work Brings the Darkness to Light — Reiki Brings the Light Into the Darkness

Shadow work is the act of facing what has long been hidden.
Reiki is the light that makes that journey navigable.

Shadow work asks:

- "What have I been carrying?"
- "What am I afraid to feel?"
- "How have I learned to hide?"

Reiki responds:

- "I will walk with you."
- "You are safe here."
- "Nothing within you is unworthy of love."

Shadow work expands consciousness.
Reiki raises frequency.

Together, they shift identity, emotional chemistry, and spiritual alignment.

The soul remembers who it is beneath the scars of survival.

8. Shadow Work Begins the Integration — Reiki Completes It

Awareness does not automatically change the emotional body.
Insights alone do not dissolve the charge behind trauma.

Shadow work reveals the source.
Reiki dissolves the energetic knots.

Shadow work brings fragments to the surface.
Reiki weaves them back into wholeness.

Shadow work acknowledges the wound.
Reiki restores the soul's coherence.

Shadow work shows us where we split.
Reiki brings us home.

WHY THIS UNION IS SO POWERFUL

When these two systems work together:

- emotional truth rises without overwhelming the heart
- inner wounds are seen with empathy
- shame dissolves instead of deepening
- trauma is processed rather than reburied
- the nervous system stays stable
- forgiveness becomes possible
- the self becomes unified

Shadow work without Reiki can be harsh.
Reiki without shadow work can become avoidance.

But together, they form a bridge:

- from fear to self-understanding
- from fragmentation to unity
- from trauma to wisdom
- from self-judgment to compassion

Reiki does not bypass the shadow
— it sanctifies it.

Shadow work does not erase the wound
— it helps us listen to it.

And when listening meets healing, inner alchemy begins.

In that alchemy, darkness does not disappear.
It becomes part of the light.

CHAPTER 2:
IDENTIFYING
THE SHADOW SELF

Chapter 2: Identifying the Shadow Self

Signs Your Shadow Is Running the Show

Shadow work begins with recognition. We cannot integrate what remains invisible. The shadow is rarely loud; it moves subtly, shaping choices, reactions, and beliefs in quiet, unconscious ways. Its presence is felt through patterns rather than declarations, through unexplained emotions rather than clear logic, and through instinctive reactions that appear before the mind has time to think.

To identify the shadow, we must observe both our inner landscape and our outward behavior — where we tense, where we defend, where we resist, and where our emotions seem disproportionate to the moment.

The shadow is not an adversary.
It is a messenger.

But when left unseen, its message expresses itself through:

- emotional projections
- self-sabotage
- triggered reactions
- relational conflict
- nervous system responses

Below are the most common signs that shadow material is rising to the surface and influencing your experiences — mentally, emotionally, energetically, and spiritually.

1. Strong Emotional Reactions That Feel "Out of Nowhere"

When emotions surge faster than your logical mind can track — especially anger, shame, fear, defensiveness, or jealousy — the shadow is often behind it.

Examples:

- sudden anger over small comments
- disproportionate hurt from casual interactions
- spiraling anxiety after feeling misunderstood
- unexpected tears when a memory is triggered

These reactions are not irrational — they are layered.

They point to:

- unmet needs
- unresolved wounds
- unprocessed memories
- ancestral imprints

Reiki awareness teaches us to pause, breathe, and trace the emotion to its energetic root.

2. Judging Qualities in Others That You Reject in Yourself

Projection is one of the most direct expressions of the shadow.

When traits in others trigger strong judgment, irritation, discomfort, or hostility, it may not be about them at all — but about the aspects of yourself you have disowned.

For example:

- criticizing someone's sensitivity while hiding your own
- condemning neediness while secretly longing for support
- resenting confidence when you fear your own visibility

What we judge externally often reflects what we cannot accept internally.

Shadow work asks:
"Where is this trait alive within me?"

Reiki softens the inquiry so it feels safe to answer.

3. Perfectionism, Self-Criticism, and Internal Hardness

When the inner voice becomes harsh, punishing, or demanding, the shadow is attempting to protect you from shame, rejection, or failure.

This may look like:

- setting impossible standards
- feeling guilt when you rest
- believing you must earn your worth
- quickly dismissing your accomplishments

The shadow tries to prevent vulnerability by controlling outcomes.

Reiki reminds you:

- you are already worthy
- you do not have to be perfect to be loved
- the inner critic is a wounded protector

Compassion begins where perfectionism ends.

4. Feeling Emotionally Numb or Disconnected

The shadow is not always intense.
Sometimes, it appears through emotional shut-down.

Signs include:

- feeling numb when others expect emotion
- withdrawing when conflict arises
- avoiding intimacy
- using busyness to escape reflection

Numbness is not the absence of emotion — it is the defense against overwhelming emotion.

This is the shadow in freeze-mode.

Reiki gently reawakens emotional sensation and returns authenticity to the heart.

5. Repeating the Same Painful Patterns

Shadow material expresses itself through cycles:

- choosing similar partners
- reliving identical conflicts
- sabotaging opportunities
- returning to familiar disappointments

These loops are unhealed imprints, replaying until they are seen, understood, and released.

Patterns are not curses — they are invitations.

Reiki brings clarity to the deeper origin:

- childhood attachment experiences
- absorbed family beliefs
- past-life emotional contracts
- karmic relational echoes

There is always a root.
Patterns guide us toward it.

6. Avoiding Certain Emotions, Topics, or Vulnerabilities

When we avoid discussing, feeling, or acknowledging specific emotions, the shadow is guarding them.

Common avoidances:

- sadness
- anger
- failure
- grief
- abandonment
- unworthiness

Avoidance is protection.

Shadow work asks:
"What do I fear would happen if I allowed myself to feel this?"

Reiki offers the safety needed to answer without collapsing into the pain.

7. Over-Identifying With a "Positive" Identity

Sometimes the shadow hides beneath spiritual persona, professional success, or constructed identity.

Examples:

- "I'm always the strong one."
- "I never get angry."
- "I'm fine, no matter what."
- "I don't need help."

When we cling tightly to an identity, it often masks wounds beneath it:

- the strong one is terrified of being seen as weak
- the peaceful one is suppressing anger
- the self-sufficient one fears abandonment

The shadow sits behind the masks we most protect.

Reiki helps dismantle identity armor with compassion rather than force.

8. Difficulty Accepting Compliments, Affection, or Support

When the shadow carries beliefs of unworthiness, receiving becomes difficult.

This may appear as:

- rejecting praise
- hiding your achievements
- downplaying abilities
- feeling uncomfortable when cared for

If love feels threatening rather than nourishing, the shadow is revealing old narratives:

- "I am not enough."
- "Love is conditional."
- "If I receive, I will owe."
- "If I am seen, I will be hurt."

Reiki dissolves emotional charge around these beliefs and communicates a deeper truth:
You are safe to receive.

9. Resistance to Stillness, Introspection, or Silence

The shadow often lives just under conscious awareness. When stillness threatens to reveal it, distraction becomes self-preservation.

Avoidance behaviors include:

- constant busyness
- compulsive productivity
- emotional detachment
- nonstop external focus

If silence feels uncomfortable, it may be because the inner voice is waiting — and the shadow knows it will finally be heard.

Reiki softens inner tension, allowing silence to feel like sanctuary rather than threat.

10. Feeling Emotionally "Triggered" by Light

Sometimes, intense discomfort arises in the presence of:

- kindness
- vulnerability
- authenticity
- someone living in their power

This discomfort is the shadow recognizing what it believes it cannot safely embody.

Triggers are not personal failures.
They are signals that integration is ready to begin.

11. The Body Speaks What the Mind Will Not

The shadow often appears through somatic signals:

- tight chest
- throat constriction
- digestive upset
- chronic tension
- fatigue
- shallow breath
- aching joints
- migraines

Where emotion was once suppressed, the body became the archive.

Reiki gently rewrites that archive through vibrational release, nervous system soothing, and energy field restoration.

THE SHADOW REVEALS ITSELF THROUGH PATTERN, NOT PUNISHMENT

The signs above are not flaws, weaknesses, or spiritual immaturity.
They are signals — invitations to self-discovery, emotional liberation, and energetic realignment.

Where psychology helps us name these patterns,
Reiki helps us meet them with compassion.

Where the shadow shows where healing is needed,
Reiki shows us how to heal without self-violence.

Shadow material surfaces when we are ready for it.
Its emergence is evidence of growth, not collapse.

A GENTLE REFLECTION

If any of these signs feel familiar, take a breath.
You are not doing anything wrong — you are becoming aware.

Awareness is the doorway.
Reiki is the light that leads you through it.

How Unconscious Patterns Form

The Emotional Blueprint Beneath Behavior

To understand the shadow self, we must first understand how our inner world is shaped. Unconscious patterns are not random habits or personality flaws — they are emotional blueprints formed by experience, environment, and instinctive survival needs.

Most of what we call "shadow" began as a strategy:

- to be safe,
- to belong,
- to be loved,
- or to avoid overwhelm.

These patterns settled quietly into the subconscious, shaping how we feel, respond, relate, and protect ourselves long before we could speak about our needs.

1. Early Conditioning and Learned Survival

Childhood is the most formative period for emotional imprinting.
In early life, the nervous system is open, sensitive, and unguarded. Experiences that feel unsafe — even in subtle ways — often become the foundation for later defense patterns.

Examples:

- A child who felt ignored learns to silence their needs.
- A child who experienced unpredictability learns to stay hypervigilant.
- A child who was judged learns to self-censor or perfect.

- A child who absorbed stress becomes the fixer or appeaser.

These responses were intelligent at the time.
They protected the child from emotional pain or relational loss.

As adults, these same adaptive strategies remain active in the subconscious, even when they no longer serve us.

2. Emotional Suppression and the Nervous System

When emotions are unsafe to express, the body stores them.

Common childhood restraints:

- "Don't cry."
- "Be good."
- "Stop making a scene."
- "We don't talk about that."

These messages teach us that natural emotional impulses must be hidden or controlled.

Over time, the nervous system learns:

- tension is safer than vulnerability
- silence is safer than honesty
- withdrawal is safer than intimacy
- compliance is safer than authenticity

These become unconscious patterns, not because we chose them, but because the body remembers what once protected us.

Reiki helps unwind this body-memory gently, allowing emotional truth to return.

3. Absorbed Family Beliefs and Energetic Inheritance

We inherit more than genetics.
We absorb emotional frequency, tone, family conditioning, and relational dynamics.

Patterns form from:

- what our caregivers modeled
- what they feared
- what they endured
- what they avoided
- what they never healed

The shadow often reflects the wounds that run through the family line:

- unworthiness
- abandonment
- silence
- perfectionism
- emotional shutdown
- guilt-based identity

These unconscious transmissions settle into the subtle body, becoming energetic programs that influence behavior without our awareness.

Reiki, especially distance work and emotional clearing techniques, can access these imprints at the energetic root.

4. Cultural and Social Conditioning

Society teaches us what is acceptable and what is not:

- gender roles
- emotional expectations
- standards of success
- religious or moral ideals
- what is "strong" or "weak"

Any natural part of our expression that conflicts with these expectations may be pushed into the shadow.

For example:

- Sensitivity may be labeled as weakness.
- Ambition may be judged as selfish.
- Sadness may be treated as instability.
- Anger may be condemned instead of understood.

The psyche learns to suppress what is unwelcome.

These suppressed expressions do not disappear — they simply go unconscious, shaping everything from boundaries to confidence to relationships.

5. Emotional Pain Without Resolution

When a painful experience occurs without comfort, validation, or emotional repair, the mind and energy field create patterns to prevent further hurt.

These patterns often include:

- emotional detachment
- emotional overfunctioning

- avoidance of intimacy
- belief that love is conditional
- mistrust
- hyper-independence
- self-sabotage

Every wound forms a rule:

- "I must not need anyone."
- "I must never fail."
- "I must always be the strong one."
- "I should stay quiet to stay safe."
- "If I get close, I will be abandoned."

Shadow work reveals these hidden rules.
Reiki dissolves them at their energetic root.

6. Protective Identity Roles

To survive emotionally, we learn roles:

- the peacemaker
- the problem-solver
- the perfectionist
- the invisible one
- the caretaker
- the achiever
- the strong one
- the silent one

These roles were armor.

But as adults, they prevent:

- honest expression
- emotional intimacy
- vulnerability
- authenticity
- self-trust

Reiki makes it safe to remove the armor gently, honoring the role while releasing its necessity.

7. Emotional Shock and Freeze States

Moments of intense emotional shock — even when brief — can freeze energy into the subconscious.

Examples:

- betrayal
- abandonment
- humiliation
- loss
- sudden fear
- unexpected rejection

The psyche stores not only the memory, but the emotional vibration and physical sensation of the moment.

Without release, the imprint becomes pattern:

- flinching at vulnerability
- rejecting help
- pulling back when love appears
- fearing loss more than pursuing joy

Reiki helps release trapped survival energy from the nervous system, allowing the body to exhale what it once held.

8. The Mind Seeks Familiarity Over Freedom

Unconscious patterns persist because the nervous system prioritizes the familiar over the unknown — even when the familiar is painful.

The subconscious believes:

- "Known pain is safer than unfamiliar possibility."

So the shadow repeats:

- the same relationships
- the same responses
- the same self-judgment
- the same fears

Reiki restores coherence and emotional capacity, allowing the body to feel safe in unfamiliar choices — the essence of real transformation.

9. Energetic Fragmentation and Self-Rejection

Whenever we reject a part of ourselves — a feeling, memory, need, instinct, sensitivity, or truth — that rejected piece becomes shadow.

Fragmentation occurs when we decide:

- "That part of me is wrong."
- "That feeling is dangerous."
- "That memory is shameful."
- "That need is unacceptable."

Reiki invites those fragments back into the heart with gentleness.

Integration replaces rejection.
Compassion replaces resistance.
Awareness replaces suppression.

The shadow was never the enemy — only the exiled.

10. Pain Becomes Identity

Over time, unhealed wounds shape how we see ourselves:

- "I am unlovable."
- "I am not enough."
- "I am too much."
- "I am alone."
- "I am broken."

These beliefs form the deepest unconscious patterns.

Reiki loosens identity attachment, reminding the subconscious that:

- pain is not personality
- trauma is not destiny
- conditioning is not the soul's truth

As energy softens, the self remembers itself beyond the wound.

PATTERNS FORM TO PROTECT YOU

Everything that lives in the shadow was created for emotional safety.

Patterns form because:

- the child needed protection
- the nervous system needed stability
- the heart needed shielding
- belonging felt essential
- rejection felt dangerous
- vulnerability felt too risky

These patterns are not weaknesses.
They are evidence of survival.

Shadow work reveals them.
Reiki helps us release, rewrite, and heal them.

REIKI'S ROLE IN UNPATTERNING THE PAST

Reiki does not erase the past.
It releases the emotional charge, energetic tension, and neurological imprint that keeps the past alive in the present.

As patterns unwind:

- the body relaxes
- the mind quiets
- reactions soften
- triggers ease
- compassion deepens

And the shadow begins to transform into wisdom.

When unconscious patterns are seen, honored, and finally allowed to dissolve gently through Reiki's compassionate current, the soul returns to its natural alignment — whole, aware, and free.

This is the beginning of remembrance, not reconstruction.

It is the return home.

Reiki Meditation: Meeting the Shadow Within

A Gentle Encounter with the Hidden Self

This meditation is designed to help you meet the shadow softly — not as a confrontation, but as a compassionate reunion. You are not entering this space to fix, control, or judge what rises. You are here to witness, listen, and extend unconditional presence.

Before beginning, remember the core truth:
The shadow is not a threat. It is a part of you that once protected something tender.

Reiki will serve as your light, your grounding, and your guide.

PREPARATION

Create a Safe Space

Choose a quiet, comfortable place where you can sit or lie down without interruption.
Dim the lights, silence devices, and allow your breath to slow.

Suggested additions:

- A candle
- A small crystal
- A journal nearby
- Soothing music or silence

You may place your hands on your heart or lap — wherever feels natural.

OPENING INTENTION

Take a slow inhale through the nose, and exhale gently through the mouth.

Silently say:

"I call upon Reiki — the universal life-force energy — to bring safety, compassion, and clarity as I meet the hidden parts of myself. I am protected. I am grounded. I am ready to listen without judgment."

Feel the words settle through your body.

HAND PLACEMENT AND REIKI ACTIVATION

Gently rest your hands in the following position:

Heart Chakra to Solar Plexus

- One hand over the sternum
- The other just beneath the ribcage

This connects:

- emotional truth (Heart)
- identity, power, and inner expression (Solar Plexus)

If you are attuned, invite Reiki to flow.
If not attuned, simply breathe and imagine a soft, warm light filling your palms.

Allow the energy to move at its own pace.

GROUNDING THE BREATH

Inhale for a count of four.
Hold for two.
Exhale for six.

Repeat this rhythm until the nervous system begins to unwind.

Feel the body soften.
Shoulders relax.
Mind quiets.

Let each breath whisper:
"I am safe."

REIKI MEDITATION: MEETING THE SHADOW WITHIN

Eyes-Open Guided Experience

As you read, allow the words to guide your awareness inward.
You do not need to close your eyes.
Simply soften your gaze, slow your breath, and let your focus drift gently into your inner world.

Move at your own pace.

Descent into the Inner Landscape

Begin by noticing your breath.
A slow inhale…
and a soft exhale.

Now bring your attention inward — away from thought, and toward the feeling space inside your chest.
Imagine your awareness travelling down from the mind and

settling into the heart center.
Just the idea of moving inward is enough.

Within your heart space, picture — or simply sense — a doorway.

There is no correct form.
Allow whatever arises:

- stone
- wood
- a doorway of light
- a sheer veil
- a simple arch
- or a doorway that is only sensation, not image

This inner doorway is the path to the shadow self —
the part of you that has been waiting patiently to be seen.

There is no force here.
Only invitation.

Whenever you feel ready, imagine yourself stepping through.

Even the slightest sense of movement is enough.

On the other side, notice what appears.

Your shadow may show itself as:

- a younger version of you
- a symbolic figure
- light or mist
- a sensation in the body
- an emotional tone
- a memory surfacing
- or simply the feeling that something is present

There is no wrong form.

The shadow reveals itself in the language that your soul understands.

Take a breath.
Observe gently.
There is no need to rush.

When you feel ready, ask inwardly:

"What do you need me to understand?"

Then wait with openness.

A response may come as:

- a word
- a feeling
- a memory
- an image
- a sensation shifting in the body
- or silence

Silence is also an answer.
It may be the shadow's way of saying,
"Thank you for coming. I am not ready to speak yet."

You are not here to demand anything.
You are here to witness truth that has been waiting to be heard.

If it feels comfortable, place both hands over your heart.
Feel warmth beneath your palms.
Imagine Reiki flowing from your hands into the space where your shadow presence stands.

Softly offer these words inwardly:

"You are safe with me now.
You no longer need to hide.
I see you. I hear you.
Thank you for protecting me.
Thank you for surviving with me."

Let warmth surround whatever appeared.
Let compassion soften the edges.

If emotion rises, allow it.
If tears form, welcome them.
If numbness lingers, accept it.

Every response is valid.

Shadow integration is gentle.

So instead of asking your shadow to transform, offer:

"When you are ready, you may come home."

Imagine Reiki as a soft glow — surrounding, comforting, welcoming — not pulling, not pushing.

Let the shadow know that return is safe.
And that transformation happens through permission, not force.

If your body feels ready, move one hand to the Solar Plexus and the other to the Sacral Chakra below the navel.

Let your breath flow into this connection.

Notice any sensation —

- tightness
- heaviness
- buzzing
- pressure
- or subtle resistance

With each exhale, imagine that sensation loosening, unraveling, dissolving.

See the shadow held in golden light —
not erased, but comforted.

Light does not destroy.
It reveals, softens, and welcomes.

Before you end, offer one final message:

"I will return to you.
You are not alone anymore."

This seals trust.
It tells the shadow that this is a relationship —
not an interrogation or extraction.

It communicates respect.

Now picture the doorway once more.
When you're ready, imagine stepping back through it — gently, without hurry.

Bring awareness back to your body:

- the length of your spine
- the sensation of your feet
- the weight of your hands
- the rhythm of your breath

Invite Reiki to settle into every cell —
quiet, warm, balancing.

Take one full inhale…
and a slow, complete exhale.

Let your gaze fully return to the room around you.

You have met a part of your inner self today.
And that alone is an act of profound healing.

OPTIONAL INTEGRATION PRACTICE

Write in your journal:

- What did I feel or sense?
- What message emerged?
- What emotion or memory surfaced?
- What part of me was asking to be seen?

If nothing came, write that too:
"I sat with myself today. That is enough."

Because it is.

ENERGETIC AFTERCARE

Shadow encounters can stir subtle emotions for hours or days. To support integration, you may:

- drink water
- ground with food
- walk in nature
- place hands on the heart again
- receive or self-channel Reiki before sleep

Honor whatever your body asks for.

A FINAL REMINDER

This meditation is not about diving into pain or exposing wounds.
It is an act of reunion.

Every shadow began as protection.
Every hidden part arose to help you survive something you could not hold alone.

You meet it now not to fix it, but to free it from isolation.

Reiki is the light that makes that reunion safe.

In time, the shadow softens, emotions unwind, and the fragmented self becomes whole — not by force, but by love.

This is the beginning of inner peace.

And the next chapter of your becoming.

CHAPTER 3:
HEALING
SELF-REJECTION
AND FEAR

Chapter 3: Healing Self-Rejection and Fear

Common Roots of Inner Rejection: Shame, Guilt, and the Fear of Being Unlovable

Before shadow work can soften the parts of us we've hidden, we must first understand why those parts were pushed away. Nearly every experience of inner rejection can be traced to three core emotional roots:

shame, guilt, and fear of being unlovable.

These inner wounds are not flaws in character — they are the echoes of moments when we did not feel emotionally safe. When the nervous system perceived vulnerability as danger, the psyche responded by dividing the self: one part shown to the world, the other exiled into silence.

Reiki invites these rejected aspects back into wholeness, not by force, but by recognizing the truth beneath every shadow wound:

Nothing within you became hidden without reason.

1. Shame: "There is Something Wrong With Me."

Shame is one of the deepest emotional imprints connected to the shadow.
It forms when a child — or an adult — interprets emotional pain as evidence of personal failure.

Instead of thinking:

- "I was hurt,"

shame says:

- *"I am the reason I was hurt."*
- *"There must be something wrong with me."*
- *"If I were better, this wouldn't have happened."*

Shame thrives where love felt withdrawn, conditional, unavailable, or unpredictable.

Common roots:

- emotional neglect
- criticism or comparison
- religious or moral pressure
- humiliation
- bullying
- abandonment
- feeling unseen or unprotected

The inner response becomes:

- self-silencing
- hiding authenticity
- fear of emotional exposure
- perfectionism

- over-achievement
- avoiding intimacy

Shame convinces the psyche that vulnerability is unacceptable, so pieces of identity are pushed into the shadow for survival.

Reiki dissolves shame not by denying it, but by teaching the inner self that worthiness is inherent — untouched by past conditions.

2. Guilt: "I Am the Cause of the Pain Around Me."

Guilt often develops when the nervous system absorbs responsibility for emotions it could not possibly control.

A child may feel guilt for:

- a parent's sadness
- a family conflict
- tension in the home
- unmet expectations
- being too much or not enough
- simply having needs

When emotional expression is unwelcome, guilt becomes the story that explains safety:

- "If I don't upset anyone, I will be loved."
- "If I stay quiet, no one will leave."
- "If I take the blame, the world will feel predictable."

Guilt creates a shadow pattern of:

- self-blame
- chronic apologizing
- emotional caretaking
- over-responsibility

- difficulty saying "no"

It also fosters the belief that joy must be earned, that love requires performance, and that worth is transactional.

Reiki softens guilt at its root by reconnecting the heart to innocence — not perfection, but purity of intention.

In the presence of Reiki, guilt melts into clarity:
You did not cause the emotional wounds around you.
You merely adapted to survive them.

3. Fear of Being Unlovable: "If They Know Me, They Will Leave."

The deepest root of inner rejection is the belief that something about us makes love unsafe or unavailable.

This fear often forms when emotional bonds were uncertain, inconsistent, or conditional. The nervous system becomes trained to predict rejection — even when safety is present.

It shows up as:

- fear of abandonment
- distrust of intimacy
- keeping relationships shallow
- envy of others' confidence
- hiding passions
- silencing needs
- feeling unworthy of support

Instead of believing
"I was hurt,"
the shadow forms the story
"I must not be lovable."

This belief can become so embedded that any moment of joy, connection, or goodwill triggers doubt — as though love must be rationed or earned.

Reiki untangles this fear by restoring access to the heart chakra — the center of receptivity, emotional truth, compassion, and connection.

Where the heart has been guarded, Reiki brings ease.
Where trust has been severed, it invites safe surrender.

Why These Wounds Become Shadows

Shame, guilt, and the fear of being unlovable all share a single instinctive purpose:

self-protection.

When a child (or adult) cannot express emotion safely, the inner self stores it.
When connection feels brittle, the inner self hides vulnerability.
When love feels conditional, the inner self divides authenticity from visibility.

The shadow becomes the vault.

It holds:

- tenderness
- grief
- unmet needs
- longing
- anger
- softness
- the desire to be seen

All of it protected until the inner world feels safe enough to be whole again.

THE ROLE OF REIKI IN HEALING SELF-REJECTION

Reiki is profoundly effective for restoring wholeness in these wounded places because it embodies what the shadow rarely received:

- unconditional presence
- non-judgment
- emotional safety
- compassionate witnessing

As Reiki flows through blocked chakras and tense emotional centers, it communicates a message that begins to rewrite the inner narrative:

"There is nothing within you that makes you unworthy of love."

Reiki softens:

- the tightness around shame
- the self-criticism born from guilt
- the walls built around unlovability

It brings warmth where the heart once contracted, and welcomes back the pieces of identity that were exiled at the moment love felt risky.

RETURNING TO SELF-ACCEPTANCE

Healing self-rejection is not about eliminating the shadow — but learning to embrace it.

Your shadow does not carry proof of unworthiness.
It carries proof of how deeply you longed for love, safety, and belonging.

Reiki helps you meet those unmet longings with compassion instead of judgment, tenderness instead of resistance.

Each layer released restores:

- emotional capacity
- self-trust
- authenticity
- inner alignment
- a deeper relationship with Spirit

The goal is not perfection.
It is reunification.

As shame dissolves, the heart opens.
As guilt softens, truth returns.
As fear of unlovability fades, the soul remembers itself.

This is the beginning of coming home — not to the mask, but to the truth beneath it.

Chakra Imbalances Associated with Self-Rejection

How Emotional Wounds Shape the Energy Field

When we speak of self-rejection, we are not speaking only of belief patterns.
Self-rejection has an energetic signature.

Emotions that were suppressed, identities that were hidden, and love that was withheld leave vibrational residue that gathers in the chakra system. Because chakras translate emotional experience into energy flow, any long-standing rejection of the self—conscious or unconscious—creates distortion, constriction, or depletion.

Whether mild or profound, self-rejection most often affects the Root, Sacral, Solar Plexus, Heart, Throat, Third Eye and Crown chakras.
Each carries a particular aspect of our identity, belonging, emotional expression, and sense of worth.
When fear, shame, or guilt settle into these centers, they transform from wounds in the psyche into energetic blockages in the subtle body.

Below is an overview of how these imbalances manifest, and what they reveal about the deeper emotional story within the shadow.

ROOT CHAKRA (MULADHARA)

Safety, Belonging, Identity

The Root Chakra governs our sense of:

- being welcome in the world
- emotional safety
- permission to exist exactly as we are
- the right to have needs, feelings, and presence

When early experiences created instability, rejection, or emotional abandonment, the Root becomes compromised.

Signs of Root Chakra imbalance from self-rejection:

- feeling unsafe in relationships
- distrust of others
- hyper-vigilance
- difficulty grounding
- fear of vulnerability
- emotional isolation
- withdrawing or dissociating

Shadow message stored here:
"I am not safe to be myself."

Reiki work to the Root chakra provides calm, grounding, and a sense of internal stability that allows shadow material to surface without overwhelm.

SACRAL CHAKRA (SVADHISTHANA)

Emotion, Sensitivity, Worthiness of Connection

The Sacral Chakra is the seat of:

- emotional expression
- vulnerability
- creativity
- sensitivity
- sensuality
- permission to feel

When guilt, shame, or punishment surrounded emotional needs, the Sacral contracts.

Signs of Sacral imbalance from self-rejection:

- emotional numbness
- feeling undeserving of love or pleasure
- difficulty receiving affection
- suppression of creativity
- fear of intimacy
- over-giving to compensate for unworthiness

Shadow message stored here:
"My emotions are a burden. My needs are too much."

Reiki softens this tightness, restoring emotional flow and bringing compassion to the vulnerable inner child.

SOLAR PLEXUS CHAKRA (MANIPURA)

Self-Worth, Confidence, Inner Power

The Solar Plexus is the energetic seat of:

- self-respect
- identity
- inner power
- self-expression
- boundaries
- personal truth

When childhood messaging implied we were not enough—too loud, too emotional, too quiet, too sensitive—this chakra absorbs those judgments.

Signs of Solar Plexus imbalance from self-rejection:

- chronic self-criticism
- perfectionism
- imposter syndrome
- difficulty speaking desires
- shrinking in relationships
- surrendering power to others
- constant self-doubt

Shadow message stored here:
"Who I am is not acceptable."

Reiki at the Solar Plexus helps dissolve self-judgment and restore internal authority.
It reminds the spirit that confidence is not arrogance—confidence is authenticity.

HEART CHAKRA (ANAHATA)

Self-Love, Acceptance, Emotional Truth

Perhaps no chakra is more deeply impacted by self-rejection than the Heart.

When love felt conditional, withheld, unpredictable, or unavailable, the Heart learned to protect itself—even from its own desires.

Signs of Heart Chakra imbalance from self-rejection:

- inability to receive love
- shutting down during emotional intimacy
- over-apologizing
- feelings of unworthiness
- rejecting compliments
- resentment rooted in unmet needs
- compassion for others, but not for oneself

Shadow message stored here:
"I must earn love. If I am truly seen, I will be rejected."

Reiki at the Heart restores compassion and connection, allowing the inner self to open again—gently, safely, and at its own pace.

THROAT CHAKRA (VISHUDDHA)

Truth, Voice, Authentic Expression

Self-rejection often silences the voice.

When the authentic self once felt unsafe to express—or expression led to punishment, shame, or abandonment—the Throat closes to protect the psyche.

Signs of Throat imbalance from self-rejection:

- fear of speaking truths
- downplaying achievements
- inability to ask for what you need
- chronic self-editing
- swallowing emotion instead of expressing it
- hiding passions, desires, or vulnerabilities

Shadow message stored here:
"My truth will cost me love. Silence keeps me safe."

Reiki at the Throat encourages gentle honesty and emotional courage, reminding the inner voice that expression is not danger—it is liberation.

THIRD EYE CHAKRA (AJNA)

Intuition, Inner Vision, Self-Trust

The Third Eye is the center of:

- inner wisdom
- intuition
- spiritual sight
- self-awareness
- discernment
- personal truth

When the shadow forms through shame, guilt, and unworthiness, the Third Eye internalizes emotional mistrust:

"I cannot trust what I feel."
"My intuition is flawed."
"My inner knowing is dangerous."

This usually stems from times when…

- instincts were dismissed
- feelings were invalidated
- subtle perception was mocked
- emotional truth conflicted with what others preferred
- a child was told their experience "didn't happen"

To survive, the psyche learned to override intuition.

Signs of Third Eye imbalance related to self-rejection:

- dismissing intuitive messages
- chronic self-doubt
- inability to make decisions
- seeking constant external validation

- intellectualizing emotions
- ignoring inner red flags
- suppressing spiritual gifts
- discounting dreams, déjà vu, or inner guidance

In shadow work, this chakra often holds blind spots — areas of the self we simply refuse to see because seeing them once felt unsafe.

Reiki here restores inner trust:

- softening doubt
- clearing mental fog
- calming fear around intuition
- helping the practitioner feel safe witnessing their truth

The Third Eye reopens when we accept that our inner knowing is not a threat — it's our greatest ally.

CROWN CHAKRA (SAHASRARA)

Spiritual Connection, Identity, Worthiness of Divine Love

The Crown Chakra governs:

- our relationship with Source
- spiritual belonging
- soul identity
- higher purpose
- unity consciousness
- the belief that we are held, guided, and supported

Self-rejection impacts the Crown as a subtle fracture:
"If I am unworthy of love from others, how could I be worthy of Divine love?"

This belief can arise from:

- religious wounds
- strict moral conditioning
- spiritual shame
- abandonment trauma
- feeling unseen or unsupported in times of pain

The Crown closes when the soul decides:

- "I am alone."
- "No higher power cares for me."
- "I'm spiritually separate or flawed."
- "I'm unworthy of guidance or protection."

Signs of Crown imbalance from self-rejection:

- feeling disconnected from Spirit or higher purpose
- difficulty trusting spiritual experiences
- existential doubt
- feeling unsupported or unseen by the Universe
- believing others are more spiritually gifted
- self-isolation in moments of emotional pain

The deepest Crown wound is spiritual loneliness — the belief that we are separate from love, unsupported by the Divine, or beneath blessing.

Reiki heals this by reconnecting the individual to:

- universal consciousness
- spiritual intelligence
- unconditional Divine compassion
- the energetic truth that *nothing in the soul is unworthy*

Where the Crown has contracted around unworthiness, Reiki gently restores luminous flow.

THE UNIFIED SHADOW PATTERN IN THE CHAKRAS

Across the energetic body, self-rejection leaves a trace — but it becomes especially potent when it reaches the Third Eye and Crown. Here, emotional wounds crystallize into spiritual doubt, identity confusion, and mistrust of inner wisdom. Yet the pattern that forms in these upper chakras is only one layer of a much larger truth:

Self-rejection is, at its core, a wound of love and belonging.

When the inner child learned that vulnerability might cost safety, affection, or acceptance, belief systems formed to protect the heart. Over time, these beliefs sank beneath awareness, weaving themselves into the chakras and shaping how energy flows.

The result is a consistent energetic pattern found anywhere self-rejection has taken root. It often includes:

- difficulty trusting intuition
- fear of inner guidance
- shame around spiritual gifts or sensitivity
- abandonment wounds projected onto the Divine
- resistance to receiving support (energetic or emotional)
- doubt in personal wisdom, purpose, and identity

When these beliefs solidify, the soul begins interpreting emotional survival strategies as spiritual truth, and the inner dialogue shifts into subtle self-abandonment:

- "I must not be chosen."
- "My intuitive experiences aren't real."
- "I am unworthy of love and connection."
- "There is something spiritually wrong with me."

Yet none of these stories are evidence — they are wounds speaking through memory.

At the deepest level, the shadow carries variations of the same fear:

- "If I am truly myself, I will be rejected."
- "My needs make me unlovable."
- "Authenticity is unsafe."

These emotional imprints tighten the Root, contract the Sacral, dim the Solar Plexus, armor the Heart, silence the Throat, veil the Third Eye, and close the Crown. The entire chakra system responds as if hiding is necessary for survival.

Energy that longs to flow becomes constricted.
Expression becomes muted.
Connection becomes distant.

The psyche and energy field both attempt to keep us safe by limiting:

- exposure,
- truth,
- vulnerability,
- spiritual openness,
- and intuitive trust.

But Reiki gently reveals what self-rejection obscured:

Worthiness was never conditional, inner truth was never flawed, and spiritual connection was never revoked.

Reiki does not impose worthiness — it uncovers it.
It softens shame, dissolves guilt, quiets fear, and reminds the heart that protection is no longer needed.

As Reiki works through the chakras, the subtle body begins to uncoil:

- the body feels safer
- the mind loosens its defenses
- the heart opens without strain
- intuition becomes trustworthy again
- spiritual connection feels real rather than imagined

And slowly, as the shadow softens, a new inner belief takes shape:

"I do not need to reject myself to stay safe."

From this place, the Third Eye clears, the Crown brightens, and every chakra begins returning to its natural expression.

Self-rejection dissolves not because the shadow disappears, but because the hidden parts were met with compassion.

Reiki becomes the bridge back to wholeness — a loving awareness that restores the simple, powerful truth:

You were never separate, never unworthy, never broken. Only misled by the echoes of pain that once taught you to hide.

And now, through remembrance, the chakras open once more.

REINTEGRATION THROUGH REIKI: ALL SEVEN CHAKRAS

The purpose of shadow healing through Reiki is not simply to clear energy, unblock flow, or awaken dormant centers — it is to reconcile every layer of the self.
Each chakra holds memories of who you needed to be in order to survive, and each carries a piece of the soul that longs to return home.

Reiki becomes the bridge.

- At the Root, where abandonment once fractured safety, Reiki restores belonging and steadiness.
- At the Sacral, where emotional truths were muted, Reiki invites feeling, creativity, and vulnerability to move freely again.
- At the Solar Plexus, where self-judgment once dimmed inner power, Reiki rekindles confidence, autonomy, and self-worth.
- At the Heart, where love was guarded, withheld, or feared, Reiki softens armor and teaches the body that connection can be safe.
- At the Throat, where silence became protection, Reiki grants voice, honesty, and the courage to express.
- At the Third Eye, where doubt clouded intuition, Reiki clears perception and restores trust in inner wisdom.
- At the Crown, where separation once felt real, Reiki reopens the channel of divine support, remembrance, and spiritual belonging.

Where shame constricted, Reiki expands.
Where guilt weighed heavily, Reiki lifts.
Where fear barricaded the heart, Reiki gently opens space.

Self-rejection becomes self-recognition.
Self-protection becomes self-trust.
What once felt like shadow becomes wisdom.

This is the alchemy of wholeness — the moment when energy work meets inner honesty.

Reintegration is not achieved by silencing wounds or erasing the past.
It comes by welcoming every exiled part back into the light, acknowledging why it hid, and letting Reiki hold it with compassion until it no longer needs to hide.

Reiki is the unconditional yes the shadow has always needed.

Its presence invites alignment — and as the seven chakras return to their natural harmony, the whole energetic field remembers what has always been true:

You are already complete.
Already worthy.
Already whole.

Reiki simply helps you feel it again.

Reiki Techniques to Open the Heart and Solar Plexus Chakras

Because the roots of self-rejection live in the stories we tell ourselves about identity and love, the Solar Plexus and Heart Chakras are central to healing shadow wounds.
When either center is imbalanced, the psyche instinctively pulls back from vulnerability, connection, confidence, authenticity, and emotional truth.

Reiki softens the defenses that formed around these chakras, allowing their natural energy to expand without force.

Below are precise, gentle techniques designed specifically for shadow integration.

1. Heart–Solar Plexus Reiki Bridge

Hands-on Healing for Worthiness and Self-Acceptance

This technique creates an energetic "bridge" between the two chakras, encouraging emotional truth (Heart) and self-identity (Solar Plexus) to communicate with each other again.

Hand Placement:

- One hand over the center of the chest (Heart)
- The other over the midpoint between sternum and navel (Solar Plexus)

Invite Reiki into both hands.

Focus on slow, grounded breath.

On each inhale, imagine energy rising from the Solar Plexus toward the Heart.
On each exhale, see compassion flowing from the Heart downward — meeting the wounded stories held in the Solar Plexus.

Intention:

"I soften the walls around my worth. I allow love to meet me where I once rejected myself."

This technique is powerful for:

- perfectionism
- self-criticism
- fear of vulnerability
- emotional numbing
- inner shame
- difficulty receiving affection

It restores communication between:

- who I am
  and
- how I allow myself to be loved.

2. The Golden Core Activation

Solar Plexus Illumination

The Solar Plexus absorbs the harshest shadow beliefs:

- "I am not enough."
- "I must earn worth."
- "I need approval to be safe."

This technique helps dissolve those energetic imprints.

Hand Placement:

- Both hands over the Solar Plexus

Visualize a warm golden light forming beneath your palms — sunlight at dawn, radiant and soft.

With each breath, see that light expand gently:

- first to the rib cage
- then into the spine
- then into the heart area
- then outward into the aura

Intention:

"I allow my inner truth to shine without fear. I am safe to be myself."

Benefits:

- strengthens confidence
- dissolves self-doubt
- eases imposter syndrome
- softens defensiveness
- reconnects personal identity to authenticity rather than performance

This activation gradually helps the Solar Plexus relax out of protection mode.

3. Heart Blooming Technique

Opening After Emotional Guarding

The Heart closes when love once felt dangerous — when vulnerability risked loss, criticism, abandonment, or betrayal.

This gentle Reiki method helps reopen it without overwhelm.

Hand Placement:

- palms lightly over the chest, fingers spread

Imagine the Heart Chakra as a flower, still but waiting.

With every inhale, picture the petals loosening.
With every exhale, see a pink-green glow expanding from the center outward.

Do not force the opening.
Let the chakra pace itself.

Intention:

"It is safe to receive love. I release the belief that I must earn my place in the world."

This technique supports:

- forgiveness
- emotional receptivity
- release of shame
- compassion toward the shadow
- openness to connection

As the Heart warms, the nervous system begins to recognize that vulnerability no longer equals threat.

4. Cross-Chakra Harmony Alignment

Balancing Power With Compassion

Self-rejection often causes an imbalance:

- some people lead from the Solar Plexus (power without softness)
- others lead from the Heart (compassion without boundaries)

This technique realigns them so neither operates alone.

Hand Placement:

- right hand over the Heart
- left hand over the Solar Plexus

Switch hands halfway through.

As Reiki flows, imagine threads of light weaving between both centers — a gentle exchange of wisdom.

The Solar Plexus offers courage and authenticity.
The Heart offers compassion and emotional truth.

Intention:

"My strength and my softness work as one. I speak from love, and I love without abandoning myself."

This practice helps:

- improve self-expression
- reduce emotional over-giving
- strengthen healthy boundaries
- balance empathy with self-respect

5. Release of Inherited Shame

Breath-Based Emotional Clearing

Many shadow beliefs were absorbed from caregivers, ancestry, culture, or religion.
This technique uses breath, Reiki, and intention to release those inherited imprints.

Hand Placement:

- Heart Chakra with one hand
- Solar Plexus with the other

As Reiki flows, inhale deeply into the solar plexus and exhale slowly through the heart.

With every breath out, imagine emotional residue leaving the energetic field:

- guilt
- judgment
- internal labels
- harsh expectations
- emotional shame

Intention:

"I return what is not mine. I release the beliefs that separated me from love."

This practice helps restore emotional authenticity by clearing root patterns of self-rejection.

6. Heart-Solar Reiki Mantra Activation

Vibrational Remembrance

Reiki amplifies sound intention.
Speaking to the chakras with clarity and compassion helps rewrite their energetic code.

Place hands wherever feels natural between the heart and solar plexus and repeat (aloud or silently):

"I am worthy of love.
I am safe in my truth.
I honor the person I am becoming."

Feel the words move into the blood, nerves, breath, and aura.

Because the shadow was born through emotional pain, vibrational re-instruction becomes medicine.

WHY THESE TECHNIQUES WORK IN SHADOW HEALING

When the Heart and Solar Plexus soften:

- emotional truth becomes less frightening
- courage rises naturally
- receiving support feels safer
- self-worth becomes internal rather than earned
- shame and guilt lose their authority

And the deeper truth resurfaces:

Rejection was never truth — only protection.

The purpose of Reiki here is not to “fix” the shadow or tear down defenses, but to show the nervous system that it no longer needs to guard the self against love.

As these two chakras reopen:

- authenticity begins to feel natural
- the body relaxes
- intuition sharpens
- relationships deepen
- and inner peace returns

This is not the end of shadow work — but it is a turning point.

Because once the Heart and Solar Plexus open to love and self-trust, the shadow no longer needs to hide.

And healing can finally begin from the inside out.

Exercise: Reiki Mirror Work Ritual

Reclaiming the Self with Compassion, Presence, and Energetic Truth

Mirror work becomes profoundly powerful when paired with Reiki.
The physical reflection of the mirror helps you meet the emotional reflection within — revealing not only what you see, but what you have believed about yourself, and what parts of you have been rejected, hidden, or forgotten.

This ritual is not a method for forcing confidence or demanding self-love.
It is an energetic witnessing.
A return to authenticity.
And an invitation for the shadow to be seen without judgment.

Approach it slowly, tenderly, and without expectation.

You are not here to affirm perfection.
You are here to recognize your wholeness.

PURPOSE OF THE RITUAL

This practice helps dissolve the inner barriers formed by:

- shame
- guilt
- unworthiness
- self-criticism
- identity-based wounds
- fear of being seen

It invites the Heart and Solar Plexus to open gently by letting you witness yourself with the same compassion that Reiki offers.

Many who do this ritual feel emotional release, quiet trembling, or unexpected stillness.
Others feel nothing at all — which is just as meaningful.

Whatever arises, it is a dialogue with your deepest self.

HOW TO PREPARE

You'll need:

- a mirror (standing, handheld, or wall-mounted)
- silence or soft music
- a private space
- 10–20 minutes

Tip:
The ritual is most effective when done slowly — reading each line, pausing, breathing, and truly seeing.

You may stand or sit. Choose what feels grounded.

Place one hand on the Heart Chakra and one on the Solar Plexus as you begin.

Take a slow breath.

Invite Reiki to flow.

Step 1 — Meeting Your Reflection

Look gently into your own eyes.

Not as critique, not as performance, not as image — but as presence.

If looking directly into your eyes feels difficult or uncomfortable, soften your gaze to the space between your brows or the bridge of your nose.
This is a natural response when the shadow has been unseen for a long time.

Breathe with yourself.

Feel your heartbeat under your hand.

Whisper silently:
"I am here."

That alone is enough to begin.

Step 2 — Inviting the Shadow Forward

As you continue to hold your gaze, imagine that behind your eyes sits the part of you that learned to hide — the part that carries childhood wounds, emotional memory, and protective armor.

Say inwardly:
"You do not need to hide from me anymore."

Observe what rises:

- a tightening in the throat
- a quiver in the stomach

- tears
- numbness
- discomfort
- tenderness
- quietness

There is no correct response.
Even resistance is communication.

Step 3 — The Reiki Release Breath

Keeping your hand placements, inhale deeply through the nose.

On the exhale, allow Reiki to flow toward the shadowed self, as though your breath carries the energy forward.

Repeat this three times — slow, steady, and present.

Between breaths, silently offer:
"I am willing to see the truth of who I am."

Watch the eyes in the mirror as you say these words.
Notice if something softens.

Step 4 — The Compassion Statement

Now speak — either aloud or silently — the following:

"I see you.
I know you've carried pain.
I know you tried to protect me.
Thank you for surviving with me."

Many people feel emotion here.
If so, place both hands over your heart.

If emotion does not come, that is also perfect.
Healing is not measured by intensity — only by honesty.

Step 5 — The Worthiness Affirmation

Return one hand to the Solar Plexus.

As you look into your own eyes, say:

"I am worthy of love, truth, and healing.
I deserve to be seen without fear."

Let these words land.

If they feel soft, open, or comforting — receive that.

If they feel false, heavy, or distant — witness that.

Either way, you are meeting yourself with truth.

Step 6 — The Silent Listening

Now… say nothing.

Simply hold your gaze and breathe.

Let your reflection tell you something without words.

Perhaps a memory flickers.
Perhaps your body communicates a sensation.
Perhaps it is simply stillness.

Trust it.

This moment is the dialogue between your conscious self and your shadow.

Step 7 — Energetic Embrace

Place both palms back over your heart and close your eyes for just one breath — but reopen them immediately after.

You are not leaving yourself.

With eyes open, visualize a warm sphere of light expanding around your reflection.
This is Reiki holding you.

Say inwardly:
"I accept you. All of you."

This phrase unlocks the Heart.
Even if only slightly.

This is the beginning.

Step 8 — Small Inquiry

When you feel ready, ask your reflection:

"What part of me still feels unworthy of love?"

You are not asking for a dramatic revelation.
Even a faint whisper of insight is enough.

If nothing surfaces, trust the silence.

Shadow work is slow alchemy.

Step 9 — The Closing Blessing

To complete the ritual, maintain eye contact and say:

"I will not abandon you.
I will return with compassion.
I will learn to love who you are."

Take one final breath with Reiki flowing through your hands, through your chest, and into the reflection of your eyes.

When you step away from the mirror, do so gently.

This ritual is a doorway, not a conclusion.

WHAT TO EXPECT AFTERWARD

Many report:

- emotional clarity
- subtle sadness
- calmness
- lightness
- old memories resurfacing
- vivid dreams
- temporary tiredness
- softening of self-judgment

You may wish to journal afterward:

- What did I feel?
- What was difficult?
- What softened?
- What felt unreachable?

Even discomfort is progress — it means the shadow has been acknowledged.

WHY THE RITUAL WORKS

Reiki offers unconditional presence.
The mirror offers true visibility.

Together, they:

- dismantle self-rejection
- soften shame
- restore emotional honesty
- open the Heart
- strengthen the Solar Plexus
- and reintroduce you to yourself with compassion

This ritual reminds the nervous system that being seen is safe.

It shows the shadow that it can exist without hiding.

It realigns the inner gaze away from judgment and toward acceptance.

And most importantly:

It turns the reflection into an encounter —
not with the surface, but with the soul.

Chapter 4:
Confronting
Emotional
Triggers
with Reiki

Chapter 4: Confronting Emotional Triggers with Reiki

What Are Emotional Triggers and How to Recognize Them

Emotional triggers are internal alarms—signals that something within us has been touched, exposed, or threatened. They often feel sudden, disproportionate, or irrational on the surface, yet they are rooted in deeply imprinted emotional memories.

A "trigger" is not the moment that hurts.
It is the wound that rises in response.

Triggers reveal the unhealed places:

- early attachment injuries
- rejection wounds
- unmet emotional needs
- internalized shame
- social conditioning
- memories we weren't ready to feel

When these wounds are contacted—by a tone, a gesture, a word, a silence, or even an energetic frequency—the nervous system lights up to protect the self.
It reacts before the conscious mind has time to understand.

Reiki allows us to meet these reactions with compassion, curiosity, and energetic safety.

UNDERSTANDING THE NATURE OF TRIGGERS

An emotional trigger is **not a flaw in character, willpower, or emotional intelligence.**
It is the nervous system recognizing a familiar threat based on past emotional imprinting.

Often, triggers activate survival responses:

- anger
- defensiveness
- withdrawal
- shutdown
- overreaction
- overthinking
- self-criticism
- people-pleasing

Each of these responses once served a purpose.
They attempted to keep the heart safe when vulnerability was associated with danger.

When we are triggered:

- the past and present moment merge
- the inner child responds instead of the adult
- fear, shame, or guilt become the internal narrator

We may intellectually know we are safe, but the body does not.
Reiki works at the level of body-memory, where triggers originate.

WHERE TRIGGERS COME FROM

Triggers are rooted in experiences where:

- our needs were dismissed
- our pain was unacknowledged
- our voice was silenced
- our love was rejected
- our boundaries were ignored
- our emotions were punished
- our identity was shamed

The shadow stores the emotional charge, while the psyche creates protective patterns.

A trigger is that charge becoming visible.

It is the shadow surfacing, saying:
"Something here feels familiar and unsafe."

When approached without judgment, triggers are full of information:

- they show us where the wound began
- they reveal what the inner child still fears
- they highlight what we have been taught not to feel
- they point to the exact place where healing is ready to begin

HOW TO RECOGNIZE EMOTIONAL TRIGGERS

Because triggers operate below conscious awareness, we recognize them not through thought, but through emotional, physiological, and energetic cues.

Here are the most common signs:

1. Disproportionate Emotional Reactions

If your emotional response is larger, louder, or heavier than the situation logically calls for, a trigger may be active.

Examples:

- sudden rage from a small comment
- deep sadness from minor disappointment
- panic over subtle misunderstanding

This is not overreaction—it is unhealed memory speaking.

2. Defensiveness or Emotional Withdrawal

Triggers often appear as:

- shutting down
- going silent
- distancing from connection
- feeling numb or cold

Withdrawal is the shadow's attempt to prevent vulnerability.

3. Tightening in the Body

The body always speaks first.

Common somatic cues:

- throat constriction
- clenched jaw
- knot in the stomach
- chest tightening
- shallow breath
- trembling or heat

- sudden exhaustion

The body mirrors the moment when the original wound occurred.

4. Flood of Self-Judgment

Triggers often awaken the internal critic.

Thoughts may suddenly arise like:

- "I'm stupid."
- "I ruin everything."
- "I'm unlovable."
- "I'm a burden."

These are not facts.
They are inherited conclusions from moments when love felt unsafe or conditional.

5. Feeling Threatened by Innocent Situations

Someone's tone, body language, or words may feel hostile or rejecting—even if logically they are not.

This happens because the nervous system responds to familiar emotional patterns, not current reality.

6. Urge to Fix, Please, or Earn Approval

Triggers often activate coping reflexes:

- apologizing excessively
- trying to control outcomes
- caretaking others' comfort
- shrinking back to avoid conflict

Beneath the reflex is fear:
"If I am too much, I will not be loved."

7. Flashbacks of Memory or Emotion

Triggers can bring up:

- a sudden image
- a childhood moment
- emotional echoes
- familiar loneliness
- déjà vu of heartbreak

Even subtle flashbacks are invitations to witness what the shadow once had to carry alone.

8. A Sense of Being "Small"

When a trigger is active, the inner child often steps forward emotionally.
We feel:

- powerless
- voiceless
- unworthy
- like we must be perfect to be safe

Recognizing this shift is profound.
It shows exactly which version of the self is asking for healing.

WHY RECOGNIZING TRIGGERS MATTERS IN REIKI WORK

Triggers are not enemies to avoid.
They are signposts pointing directly to the shadow wounds seeking integration.

To the untrained eye, triggers appear disruptive.
To the healer, they are maps.

When we understand triggers through Reiki:

- we soften instead of react
- we respond instead of collapse
- we observe instead of judge

Triggers then become portals:

- to memory
- to self-knowledge
- to emotional release
- to chakra restoration
- to inner reconciliation

The moment of activation becomes the moment of awakening.

REIKI'S ROLE IN TRIGGER AWARENESS

Reiki creates the safety needed to stay present when shadow material rises.

Its vibration:

- lowers defensive reactivity
- relaxes the sympathetic nervous system
- opens emotional pathways

- softens the energetic charge
- restores a sense of inner support

When Reiki flows during or after a trigger, the body receives a powerful message:

"You are safe enough to feel this now."

Instead of suppressing, collapsing, or projecting, we can sit with the emotion long enough to understand its origin and its purpose.

In this awareness, triggers shift from explosions to revelations.

A TRIGGER IS THE SHADOW ASKING TO BE SEEN

When we are triggered, our system is not failing — it is remembering.

And remembrance is the first step toward release.

Reiki transforms that moment of emotional disruption into a doorway:

Away from instinctive defense,
and into conscious healing.

The trigger is the knock.
Reiki is the light that lets us finally open the door.

Using Reiki to Pause, Center, and Respond Instead of React

A trigger usually pulls us into the past before we have time to understand what's happening.
Our chest tightens, thoughts sharpen, the body contracts, and an old survival pattern is activated.
In these moments, the shadow takes the wheel, not because it wants to hurt us — but because it believes it must protect us.

Reiki interrupts that reflex.

It gives the body and psyche enough safety, breath, and energetic grounding to pause long enough to choose a response rather than fall into an unconscious reaction.

Reiki becomes the energetic buffer that allows presence.

1. The Reiki Pause: Creating Space Before Reaction

When a trigger strikes, the first instinct is to react.
Reiki invites us to pause instead — even for just one breath.

Place a hand anywhere that feels grounding:

- over the heart
- solar plexus
- sacral area
- upper chest
- or simply at your side

Even a subtle touch activates regulation.

Close your eyes if possible.
If not, soften your gaze.

Let Reiki flow through the palms.

Inhale slowly.
Exhale fully.

This tiny moment of stillness disengages the emotional autopilot and gives you permission to feel without collapsing into the past.

The nervous system shifts from:

- *defense*
  to
- *curiosity*

Reiki creates space — and space is what makes conscious response possible.

2. Centering Awareness in the Present Moment

A trigger pulls the mind into an old story:

- abandonment
- shame
- guilt
- betrayal
- inadequacy

Reiki brings you back into the now.

Imagine energy descending down the spine into the Root Chakra.

This reconnects you to the present moment, reminding the body that it is safe *here*, even if it wasn't safe *then.*

As Reiki flows, quietly name what is happening:

- "I feel heat in my chest."
- "My stomach is tight."
- "I feel pulled back in time."
- "This sensation belongs to an earlier version of me."

Naming sensations instead of interpreting them interrupts the emotional narrative.

Instead of believing:
"I am unsafe,"

you begin to realize:
"I am activated."

This awareness opens the door to response.

3. Softening the Emotional Charge with Breath and Energy

Triggers become overwhelming when energy surges without outlet.

Place both hands over the Solar Plexus and breathe into the tension.

Visualize Reiki gently loosening tightness, heat, or pressure.

On the inhale:
receive support.
On the exhale:
release emotional static.

The goal is not to erase the emotion, but to reduce its intensity so the inner voice can speak with clarity.

Reiki turns emotional turbulence into emotional information.

4. Listening to the Shadow Instead of Burying It

Once regulated, ask yourself:
"What is this emotion trying to protect in me?"

This reframes reaction into inquiry.

Often the answer is:

- "A painful memory."
- "A hidden need."
- "A part of me that once felt unworthy."
- "A younger version of myself."

Reiki provides enough safety for honesty.

We shift from:

- *"Why am I like this?"*
  to
- *"What is this showing me?"*

Reaction becomes revelation.

5. Choosing Communication Over Defense

Once the emotional current has softened, Reiki supports the ability to express needs clearly instead of defending wounds unconsciously.

Instead of:

- shutting down
- attacking
- escaping
- people-pleasing
- collapsing into self-blame

The body is regulated enough to say:

- "I felt something activate in me."
- "I need a moment."
- "I'm remembering an old feeling."
- "I want to share what came up."

Reiki gives language to experiences that once felt unspeakable.

When the emotional charge is softened, communication becomes possible — with others and with ourselves.

6. Seeing the Triggered Self Through Compassionate Eyes

The moment you pause, breathe, and allow Reiki to flow, you step out of self-condemnation and into self-compassion.

Instead of:

- "I shouldn't feel this."
- "I'm too sensitive."
- "I'm weak."

the internal tone shifts to:

- "I'm hurting."
- "This makes sense."
- "Something in me wants healing."

Reiki helps the shadow feel safe enough to surface without shame.

And what is safe to feel becomes safe to transform.

7. Responding from Wholeness Rather Than Fragmentation

The goal is not to eliminate triggers, but to transform our relationship with them.

When Reiki is present, response begins to look like:

- emotional breath instead of emotional eruption
- curiosity instead of judgment
- boundaries instead of avoidance
- honesty instead of silence
- reflection instead of self-punishment

Reiki rewires the moment.

Instead of the trigger controlling the narrative,
awareness becomes the anchor.

Reaction is the shadow acting alone.
Response is the whole self — conscious, grounded, compassionate, and empowered.

THE MOMENT OF CHOICE IS THE MOMENT OF HEALING

Using Reiki in the midst of activation sends a profound message through the body:

"I am safe to feel. I am safe to stay. I do not need to abandon myself."

Over time, triggers lose their sharpness.
The nervous system learns wholeness.
The shadow learns to trust the light.

And emotional reaction begins to evolve into conscious transformation.

This is how a trigger becomes a teacher.

This is how Reiki turns old pain into present wisdom.

This is the alchemy of self-awareness —
healing at the exact moment the wound attempts to protect you.

Aura Scanning and Trigger Point Release

Reading the Field, Releasing the Charge

Because emotional triggers live within both the psyche and the energy body, they often show up first in the aura as density, tension, stagnation, heat, pressure, or contraction.
Before the conscious mind recognizes that a trigger has been activated, the field already knows — and reveals it.

Aura scanning allows the practitioner (or the individual working on themselves) to detect energetic disturbances linked to shadow wounds. Trigger Point Release then helps gently dissolve those disturbances, giving the emotional body space to unwind instead of react.

Together, these techniques help us track shadow imprints and ease the energetic charge they carry.

UNDERSTANDING AURA IMPRINTS FROM TRIGGERS

When emotions are suppressed, the unresolved energy doesn't disappear — it settles into the subtle field.
That field becomes the archive of:

- unfinished experiences
- unspoken truths
- grief we never voiced
- fear we swallowed
- needs we abandoned
- shame we inherited
- memories we learned to silence

Every trigger is the resurfacing of one of these archived imprints.

Aura scanning helps us locate where that imprint is stored.

1. Aura Scanning for Emotional Charge

In a trigger response, the aura often reveals:

- warmth or heat in certain zones
- pulsing or vibration
- dense "static" pockets
- temperature drops
- uneven flow
- energetic "walls"
- sudden collapse or weakness

How to Scan

Hand Position:

- Hover hands 2–6 inches above the body
- Begin at the Crown and move slowly downward
- Move front, back, and sides if possible

Pace:

Slow, steady, intuitive — as though your palms are listening.

Focus Areas Linked to Triggers:

- heart and lungs
- stomach/spleen
- diaphragm
- throat
- solar plexus
- upper back and shoulders

When the hands pass through a region of disturbance, the sensation changes.
It may feel:

- thicker
- denser
- hotter
- sharper
- tingling
- resistant
- emotionally "alive"

This is the energetic fingerprint of a trigger.

2. Interpreting the Sensation

Each sensation carries meaning.

Heat

Often indicates emotional inflammation: anger, humiliation, shame, injustice.

Coldness

Suggests withdrawal, numbness, emotional shutdown.

Dense or Heavy Pockets

Stored grief, guilt, or intense emotional memory.

Tingling or Buzzing

Energy trying to move but constrained by resistance or fear.

Pressure or Tightness

Identifies places where authenticity was suppressed and truth was swallowed.

These signals are not problems — they are doorways to healing.

They show where emotional energy is asking to be released.

3. Trigger Point Release Through Reiki Touch

Once the imprint is located, place the hands directly on or just above the point of tension.
Allow Reiki to flow steadily and without force.

Breath Technique:

- Inhale into the area
- Exhale down and outward as if releasing emotional weight

Energetic Intention:

"I soften the resistance here. I allow truth to be felt without fear."

As the trigger point releases, sensations may shift:

- tightness melting
- heat cooling
- emotion rising
- breath deepening
- muscles relaxing
- heaviness lifting

This is evidence of emotional charge dissolving out of the field.

4. Supporting Emotional Release Safely

Trigger points may hold memories.
Sometimes tears arise, shaking begins, or a suppressed emotion surfaces.

The practitioner's role — whether working on others or self — is not to push release, but to hold safety.

If the emotional charge is strong, place one hand on the Solar Plexus and the other on the Heart.
This regulates the nervous system while the aura clears.

Silently offer:
"I am safe to feel this. I do not need to rush."

Reiki knows how much to release and at what pace.

5. Symbol Support for Trigger Imprints

(optional for attuned practitioners)

For Level II or above:

- Sei He Ki helps soften emotional memory.
- Hon Sha Ze Sho Nen reaches trauma stored in past timelines.
- Dai Ko Myo brings spiritual light into dense imprints.

Symbols should be used with reverence, not as force.

Their role is to illuminate, not extract.

6. The After-Release State

When a trigger point clears, the aura becomes noticeably lighter in that region:

- flow increases
- warmth returns to the field
- mind feels quieter
- emotions soften
- breath deepens

Some feel sudden peace, others a gentle exhaustion.
Some feel clarity, others emptiness — as though a space once occupied by pain is finally open.

This is normal.

Emotional architecture in the field has shifted.

WHY AURA WORK MATTERS IN SHADOW HEALING

Trigger work is not purely psychological.
It is energetic.

The aura records the impact of every moment when the self felt:

- unsafe
- unseen
- invalidated
- unloved
- ashamed
- too much
- not enough

Aura scanning reads the record.
Trigger point release writes a new one.

It tells the body:
"I can feel this without breaking.
I can release this without losing myself.
I am safe now."

Reiki transforms what was once a raw activated response into:

- recognition
- compassion
- spaciousness
- sovereignty

And the same trigger that once hijacked the nervous system becomes a sacred messenger.

THE SHADOW SPEAKS THROUGH THE AURA FIRST

Emotional pain leaves energetic footprints long before the conscious mind notices anything is wrong.

When we scan the aura during triggers, we find imprints of:

- beliefs
- memories
- unmet needs
- emotional truths the shadow was forced to carry

Reiki frees those imprints gently, safely, and respectfully.

In this, aura work becomes more than technique —
it becomes the art of listening to emotional history in its purest form:

the energy it left behind.

Case Study: Healing a Betrayal Wound

A Realistic Example of Trigger Awareness and Reiki Integration

Betrayal wounds are among the most powerful roots of shadow formation.
They can come from broken trust, abandonment, deception, emotional neglect, or promises that were not kept.
When unresolved, betrayal becomes a template through which the nervous system interprets relationships.

Below is a composite case example that reflects common patterns observed in Reiki shadow-work sessions.

Names and details are changed, but the emotional truth is accurate.

CLIENT BACKGROUND

Ava, age 36, sought Reiki due to recurring patterns in relationships.
She withdrew emotionally whenever someone got close.
Praise made her uncomfortable.
Affection felt threatening.
She apologized excessively and felt deep worry whenever someone took time to respond to her.

Her trigger episodes came with:

- stomach tension
- chest pressure
- racing thoughts
- sudden distrust
- fear of abandonment

Ava knew these reactions were "too strong" for the moment, but she felt powerless to stop them.

Through intake reflection, she identified childhood wounds:

- a parent who frequently broke emotional promises
- inconsistent presence
- conditional affection

She had internalized a core belief:
"If I rely on someone, I will eventually be hurt or left."

This belief lived in the shadow and controlled her nervous system during moments of connection.

THE TRIGGER MOMENT

During her second Reiki session, Ava described a recent emotional spiral:

Someone she was dating had gone quiet for several hours. Nothing hostile occurred — no conflict, no words exchanged.

Yet Ava experienced:

- tight stomach
- shame
- obsessive worry
- fear that she had said something wrong
- an urge to apologize
- a deep need to disconnect before she could be "abandoned"

This was her shadow reacting to the *possibility* of betrayal.

In reality, her date was busy at work.
But her body remembered another time when silence meant emotional harm.

The trigger was not the silence.
The trigger was memory.

AURA SCAN AND ENERGETIC FINDINGS

As the session began, the practitioner scanned her aura.

Solar Plexus Field:

- dense pressure
- heat
- a feeling of being "coiled" or braced

Heart Chakra Field:

- pulsing at the front center
- constriction along the back of the heart, between the shoulder blades
- emotional static (a sign of unreleased grief)

Throat Chakra Field:

- muted and cool
- a slight energetic "collapse," linked to self-silencing and fear of speaking needs

These patterns are common when betrayal wounds have shaped identity.

The field reflected emotional messages the shadow was still carrying:

- "I must manage myself to stay safe."
- "Do not express needs."
- "It's safer not to depend on anyone."

REIKI INTERVENTION

Hand Placement

- One hand over the Solar Plexus
- One hand over the Heart

This placement addressed:

- fear of vulnerability
- self-protection
- unworthiness
- constriction around emotional truth

Within minutes, Ava's breathing deepened.
Tension around the diaphragm began to ease.

As Reiki flowed, emotion rose — first as tight throat pressure, then as unexpected tears.

The practitioner guided her to breathe slowly into the emotion instead of resisting it.

SHADOW REVELATION

When Ava felt calm enough, she was invited to tune inward:

"Where in your life did silence first feel like danger?"

Almost instantly, a memory surfaced:

She recalled coming home from school at age 9 after a conflict, seeking reassurance and repair, only to be met with complete emotional withdrawal.

That silence had lasted days.

To her child-mind, silence became punishment.
Proof that love was conditional.
A warning that mistakes cost belonging.

Her shadow had formed its rule that day:
"If there is distance, it means I have lost love."

Every trigger since then had activated that same rule.

ENERGETIC RELEASE AND INTEGRATION

The practitioner continued with:

- Heart–Solar Reiki Bridge
- slow breathwork
- verbal validation

As the energy softened, Ava reported:

- chest "opening"
- warmth replacing pressure
- a sense of gentleness toward herself
- fewer self-blaming thoughts

A moment of clarity emerged:
"I was afraid of losing love before I ever had the chance to receive it."

This insight signaled integration:
the shadow no longer wanted to hide this truth.

REWRITING THE INNER NARRATIVE

The practitioner guided Ava to place one hand on her heart and speak softly:

"I survived a silence that overwhelmed me.
That was then.
I am safe now."

She felt emotional relief and unexpected compassion for the younger self who endured uncertainty without support.

The betrayal wound began to shift from:

- *pain*
  to
- *understanding*

from:

- *self-defense*
  to
- *self-connection*

She no longer saw her trigger as irrational, but as intelligent: a protector responding to an echo from childhood.

AFTER-SESSION REFLECTION

In the following days, Ava noticed:

- triggers still arose
- but their intensity was lower
- her breath stayed steadier
- her body remained more grounded
- she could pause before spiraling

- she could talk about feelings instead of apologizing for them

Most importantly:
she no longer assumed abandonment the moment silence appeared.

Instead of fear, she felt curiosity.

Instead of collapse, she felt presence.

The shadow loosened.

Reiki had softened the internal alarm long enough for truth to be seen.

KEY TAKEAWAYS FROM THIS CASE

1. A trigger is rarely about the present event.

It is a memory pattern from the past replaying through the nervous system.

2. Aura scanning reveals where emotional imprints are stored.

In Ava's case: Solar Plexus, Heart, and Throat.

3. The body communicates before the mind understands.

Tightness, heat, and collapse are the shadow speaking.

4. Reiki does not erase the wound — it creates safety.

Safety allows the shadow to reveal the original pain that shaped the trigger.

5. Integration is gradual.

Ava still had triggers, but she no longer feared them.
She saw them as messages from an unhealed moment asking for compassion.

THE CORE LESSON

A betrayal wound becomes a shadow when the inner child internalizes betrayal as personal failure.

Reiki brings that frozen moment back into the light.

It tells the body:
"You are no longer alone in this memory."

The nervous system relaxes.
Self-blame unwinds.
Trust begins to return.

And bit by bit, the belief shifts from:
"I will be abandoned,"
to
"I survived something painful, and I can receive love now."

This is the heart of shadow healing:

Not erasing what happened —
but liberating the self from the story that formed around it.

CHAPTER 5:
EMBRACING
YOUR
SHADOW SELF

Chapter 5: Embracing Your Shadow Self

The Healing Power of Acceptance

Shadow work reaches its most profound turning point when we stop trying to change ourselves and begin learning to accept the parts that never felt welcome.

For many, this is the hardest lesson of all.

From childhood onward, we learn to earn love by performing, conforming, pleasing, apologizing, or hiding. We internalize the belief that only certain versions of ourselves are worthy of connection. In that system, rejection becomes protection. The shadow is born not because we are flawed, but because we learned that authenticity is dangerous.

Reiki becomes the balm that softens this inherited fear.

Its frequency carries neutrality — a pure, nonjudgmental embrace that reminds the body what unconditional presence feels like. When we bring Reiki to the shadow self, we are offering that same acceptance to the parts of us that were once exiled.

Acceptance does not mean agreeing with harmful behavior, denying pain, or romanticizing the past.
It means acknowledging our internal truth without punishment.

It is the inner voice that says:

- "I will no longer abandon you."
- "You were doing the best you knew how."
- "You have always deserved to exist."

In this moment of energetic compassion, something profound happens inside the psyche:
the shadow stops hiding.

WHY ACCEPTANCE HEALS WHERE RESISTANCE CANNOT

Everything that lives in the shadow was pushed there by pressure — fear, shame, judgment, or threat.
So long as we resist these parts, we reenact the same conditions that exiled them.
We repeat the emotional environment that forced them underground.

Resistance tells the shadow:

- "You are a problem."
- "You're embarrassing."
- "If I expose you, I'll lose love."
- "You shouldn't exist."

So the shadow remains buried, loyal to its purpose: protection at any cost.

Acceptance tells a different story:

- "You can come forward."
- "I can sit with this."
- "You're not unsafe anymore."

When the nervous system finally feels that safety, repressed emotions return to the surface.
Old beliefs soften.
Inner parts that once guarded and defended relax for the first time.

Acceptance is the key that unlocks the inner exile.

HOW REIKI FACILITATES ACCEPTANCE

Reiki holds a frequency of unconditional allowance.
It does not push trauma out of the body.
It does not demand emotional release.
It does not punish resistance.

It simply sits with what is, without agenda.

In this space:

- trembling turns into breath
- shame dissolves into truth
- anger transforms into clarity
- grief becomes devotion
- numbness becomes softness

Reiki shows us what it feels like to stand in the presence of a wound without tightening against it.

Many students and practitioners report the same moment of awakening during this phase of healing:
They begin to feel compassion for the version of themselves that had to create the shadow in the first place.

That realization alone is medicine.
It marks the moment when survival no longer needs to be the architect of identity.

ACCEPTANCE IS NOT PASSIVE — IT IS ALCHEMICAL

Most people mistake acceptance for resignation.
But in shadow work, acceptance is the fire of transformation.

When the shadow is met with compassion instead of force:

- distortions correct themselves
- defensive behaviors soften
- emotional triggers lose urgency
- inner conflict dissolves
- authenticity grows

What once felt like darkness reveals itself as a part of the psyche that was never given a chance to be seen, heard, or understood.

Reiki simply holds the space for that revelation.

From that place, the shadow begins to reorganize itself into something new:
wisdom, empathy, insight, intuition, creativity, and personal power.

This is what happens when healing shifts from fixing to welcoming.

THE ROLE OF SELF-FORGIVENESS

True acceptance cannot exist without forgiveness.
Not the kind that condones harm, but the kind that recognizes the innocence within every wound.

Self-forgiveness says:

- "I am no longer punishing myself for how I coped."
- "I understand why I reacted the way I did."
- "The behaviors that grew from hurt were adaptations — not flaws."

Reiki deepens this message through sensation.
As energy flows, the body remembers what compassion feels like.
The inner voice softens.
Survival strategies begin to loosen their grip.

The shadow doesn't need punishment.
It needs presence.

INTEGRATION BEGINS WITH BELONGING

Every part of the self longs for belonging.
The shadow is no exception.

When you sit with the shadow — not to dissect it, but to say "You may exist here" — the psyche begins to reorganize itself around wholeness rather than fragmentation.

The lesson becomes clear:

Healing does not ask us to banish the shadow.
It asks us to bring it home.

Through acceptance, we reclaim lost pieces of the self.
Through Reiki, we infuse them with light.

We stop being divided against ourselves.

And in that unity, fear becomes clarity, pain becomes insight, and the parts we once believed were unlovable reveal themselves as guardians, messengers, and teachers.

This is the power of acceptance in Reiki-based shadow work:

It reintroduces us to the parts of ourselves we thought we needed to hide — and shows us that they were never a threat. They were evidence of our strength.

Ritual: Reiki Shadow Embrace

A Hands-On Chakra Ritual for Meeting What You Once Rejected

This ritual honors the moment when you no longer run from the shadow —
when you choose presence over avoidance, compassion over self-judgment, and awareness over suppression.

It can be done seated, lying down, or in meditation posture.
Move slowly.
Feel everything.

Each hand placement is intentional.
Each breath is an invitation.
Each moment is a softening.

You are not trying to fix the shadow, change it, or force it to heal.
You are simply meeting it — and allowing it space to exist.

Step 1 — Centering the Energy Field

Hands: One palm over the Heart Chakra, one over the Solar Plexus.

Close your eyes or soften your gaze.
Feel the warmth of your palms meeting your body.

Breathe deeply:

- Inhale into the chest
- Exhale through the belly

Let Reiki flow through your hands, steady and gentle.

Silently say:
"I am here. I am willing to meet what I once hid."

This hand placement harmonizes emotional truth (Heart) and identity wounds (Solar Plexus), the two centers where self-rejection imprints most intensely.

Step 2 — Calling the Shadow Forward

Keep the hands where they are or move one to the Sacral.

Invite the shadow to rise:
Thoughts, sensations, resistance, numbness, or memory.

Whisper:
"You may come forward now. You are safe with me."

The Sacral Chakra holds:

- emotional suppression
- swallowed truth
- unmet needs
- repressed memories

Touch here signals that the body no longer needs to hold pain alone.

Step 3 — Softening Armor at the Heart

Hands: Both palms on the chest, one over the Heart, one over the upper sternum.

Inhale into the heart space.
Release tension on the exhale.

Send Reiki into every place that once feared vulnerability:

- the moments when love felt conditional
- the times authenticity led to pain
- the memories where tenderness was not safe

Silently say:
"My heart is strong enough to feel."

Let the shadow sense that truth.

Step 4 — Clearing Old Narratives at the Solar Plexus

Hands: Both palms over the Solar Plexus.

Breathe into the diaphragm — slow, steady, aware.

Feel the hand placement melt tightness, heat, or pressure.

Say:
"I release the belief that I must reject myself to be safe."

This is the chakra of self-worth, autonomy, and inner power — often the first place shadow beliefs take root.

Reiki here untangles the energy of:

- shame
- guilt
- inadequacy
- self-condemnation

Let the energy unwind.

Step 5 — Restoring Truth at the Throat

Hands: One over the Throat Chakra, other over Solar Plexus or Heart.

This communicates to the shadow that expression is allowed.

Silently offer:
"I am safe to speak truth.
My voice does not threaten belonging."

If emotion rises, let it.
If nothing happens, stay with the breath.

Reiki loosens the energetic grip of:

- self-silencing
- fear of being misunderstood
- pressure to be "acceptable"

The throat begins to soften into honesty.

Step 6 — Reconnecting to Inner Wisdom at the Third Eye

Hands: Light touch or hover over the brow.

Imagine Reiki clearing fog from inner vision.

Whisper:
"I am willing to see myself clearly."

This chakra often holds:

- self-doubt

- distorted perceptions
- fear of intuition

Shadow emotions live here as blind spots — beliefs we mistake for truth.

Let Reiki dismantle illusion gently, without force.

Step 7 — Inviting Divine Belonging at the Crown

Hands: Hover over the Crown or rest lightly on the head.

Breathe into the sensation of support.

Silently say:
"I am held by something greater than my wounds."

This step helps dissolve the spiritual abandonment imprint — the belief that past pain means spiritual disconnection.

Reiki reminds the nervous system that love and belonging are inherent, not earned.

Let the field open.

Step 8 — Integration: The Full Embrace

Return hands to the Heart and Solar Plexus.

Feel the body, the breath, the shadow, and the present moment all sharing the same space.

Say aloud or within:
"Thank you for protecting me.
You survived what I could not face.

You carried what I could not feel.
You may rest now."

This acknowledgement is the deepest alchemy of shadow work: recognizing that every fragmented part was trying to keep you safe.

Step 9 — Sealing the Aura with Light

Hover both hands a few inches above the body from Crown to Root, slowly sweeping the full length.

Visualize Reiki forming a soft cocoon of light.

Whisper:
"I am whole. Nothing within me is against me."

Let the aura feel:

- complete
- contained
- protected
- loved

Step 10 — Returning to the Present

Release all hand positions.
Place palms together at the heart.

One last breath, deep and full.

Say:
"I welcome all parts of myself home."

When ready, open the eyes.

MEANING OF THE RITUAL

This practice is not a command for the shadow to dissolve.
It is an invitation for the exiled parts of the psyche to sit at the table of consciousness.

Through touch, presence, and Reiki flow, you communicate what every shadow longs to hear:

- "You may exist."
- "You are safe now."
- "You make sense."
- "You did nothing wrong."

Acceptance replaces judgment.
Safety replaces suppression.
Integration replaces fragmentation.

And the parts that once felt like darkness begin to reveal themselves as wisdom, sensitivity, strength, intuition, and emotional intelligence.

Shadow work ends not with conquest, but with embrace.

Reiki is the light that allows that embrace to happen.

Journal Prompts: Shadow Archetypes

The Victim ◇ The Saboteur ◇ The Inner Critic ◇ The Addict

Shadow archetypes are energetic patterns born through pain, conditioning, and survival. They are not failures of character — they are adaptations developed to protect the psyche from emotional harm.

This journaling practice invites dialogue with the shadow, helping it step out of secrecy and into understanding. Approach these prompts slowly, with Reiki flowing through the hands or heart center as you write.

There are no "wrong" answers — only revelations waiting to be seen.

1. The Victim

Shadow Root: helplessness, abandonment, emotional injury, unmet needs

Core Wound:

"I am powerless. Something outside of me must change before I can feel safe."

The Victim archetype forms when someone learned early in life that they did not have the power, voice, or support needed to protect themselves. It carries grief, disappointment, and stories of emotional deficit.

Journal Prompts

- When in my life did I first feel powerless, unseen, or unprotected?
- What situations today activate that same feeling?
- How does my body respond when I believe "I can't do anything about this"?
- What benefits or safety does this archetype give me?
- What part of me is asking for help, protection, or comfort?
- If Reiki could speak through this wound, what would it want me to know?
- What truth feels stronger than any story of powerlessness?

Reiki Reflection:

Place a hand on the Solar Plexus and ask:
"Where in my life can I reclaim sovereignty without self-punishment?"

2. The Saboteur

Shadow Root: fear of success, fear of vulnerability, fear of change

Core Wound:

"If I succeed, I will be exposed, judged, or abandoned."

The Saboteur sabotages potential — not because it seeks failure, but because failure feels safer than risk. If something goes wrong by choice, the psyche doesn't have to face the pain of loss.

Journal Prompts

- In what areas of my life do I hold back, procrastinate, or undermine my own progress?
- What outcome feels threatening if I succeed?
- What deeper fear hides beneath avoidance? (rejection, expectation, judgment, loss)
- What past moment taught me that visibility or success could hurt?
- What is the Saboteur protecting me from?
- What would I choose if fear were not present in this decision?
- If Reiki could dissolve one layer of resistance today, which would I want it to be?

Reiki Reflection:

Hands over the Heart and Solar Plexus, whisper:
"I am safe to expand. Success does not threaten love."

3. The Inner Critic

Shadow Root: perfectionism, unrealistic standards, conditional self-worth

Core Wound:

"I must be perfect to be accepted. If I fail, I will lose love."

The Inner Critic is born when love or approval felt tied to achievement, control, performance, or emotional suppression. It polices behavior to prevent shame.

Journal Prompts

- What standards do I hold myself to that feel impossible or exhausting?
- Whose voice does the Inner Critic sound like?
- What am I trying to avoid through self-judgment? (humiliation, rejection, disappointment)
- What emotion sits beneath my harshest self-criticism?
- When did I learn that mistakes were dangerous?
- How does my Inner Critic think it is helping me?
- If Reiki wrapped this voice in compassion, what would change in how I speak to myself?

Reiki Reflection:

Hand on the Heart:

"I release the belief that I must earn my own acceptance."

4. The Addict

Shadow Root: emotional overwhelm, longing for relief, unprocessed pain

Core Wound:

"I need something external to numb what I feel inside."

This archetype is not limited to substances — it can be emotional escape through work, food, fantasy, relationships, perfectionism, spirituality, productivity, or performance.

Its root is self-protection.

Journal Prompts

- How do I distract myself from discomfort, vulnerability, or emotional truth?
- What sensation, belief, or memory am I avoiding when I reach for comfort or escape?
- What unmet emotional need hides beneath my compulsions?
- Which emotions feel unsafe for me to sit with?
- What was modeled to me about emotional expression or self-soothing?
- What would my pain say if it knew I would not abandon it this time?
- How can Reiki help me stay present with sensation instead of numbing it?

Reiki Reflection:

Hands over the Sacral and Solar Plexus:
"I am safe to feel. My emotions are not a threat."

5. The Controller

Shadow Root: fear of uncertainty, hyper-responsibility, survival through control

Core Wound:

"If I do not control outcomes, something painful will happen. I must stay alert."

The Controller archetype is born when chaos, unpredictability, or emotional instability were once lived experiences.
It learns that safety depends on managing everything — emotions, people, environment, image, relationships, and even spiritual expression.

Control becomes protection.
Rigidity becomes armor.

Underneath the surface is a nervous system bracing for impact.

Journal Prompts

• Where in my life do I feel hyper-responsible for others' actions, emotions, or wellbeing?
• What situation in the past taught me that losing control was dangerous?
• When I feel anxious, what do I try to tighten, plan, or regulate?
• What fear rises if I imagine allowing life to unfold without control?
• Which emotions do I avoid by staying busy, organized, or in charge?
• What is the Controller trying to prevent from happening?
• What would shift if I trusted that I was supported even without micromanaging?

Reiki Reflection

Hands on the Solar Plexus & Crown:
*"I release the belief that safety requires control.
I am guided, supported, and held by something greater than fear."*

6. The Pleaser

Shadow Root: fear of rejection, abandonment, or emotional withdrawal

Core Wound:

"If I keep others happy, I will not be left behind. Love must be earned."

The Pleaser archetype forms when acceptance felt conditional — when love, approval, or emotional stability depended on compliance.
This shadow abandons its own needs to prevent disapproval, conflict, or loss.

It smiles to mask discomfort.
It sacrifices authenticity to avoid distance.
It says "yes" to avoid being forgotten.

Underneath is a heart longing to be chosen without conditions.

Journal Prompts

- When did I first learn that my needs were secondary to others?
- In what relationships do I suppress truth, boundaries, or emotion?
- What do I fear might happen if I disappoint someone?
- How do I trade self-betrayal for temporary peace?
- What resentment or exhaustion lives beneath my people-pleasing?
- If I trusted that I did not need to perform for love, what would I say, want, or choose?
- How does the Pleaser believe it is keeping me safe?

Reiki Reflection

Hands over the Heart and Throat:

"My truth is worthy of expression.
Love is not contingent on self-erasure."

CLOSING INTEGRATION PROMPT (ALL ARCHETYPES)

Sit quietly for several breaths with one hand on the Heart and one on the Solar Plexus.

Write freely in response:
"What do these parts want from me now that I understand them better?"

Let whatever arises come without censorship.

Because the truth is simple:

Each archetype is a wounded messenger
carrying one request —

"Please do not leave me alone with this anymore."

Reiki offers them presence.
Your awareness offers them belonging.
And integration begins where exile ends.

Chapter 6:
Healing Inner
Conflict and
Self-Sabotage

Chapter 6: Healing Inner Conflict and Self-Sabotage

How Fragmented Parts Sabotage Success, Love, and Growth

Self-sabotage is not a character flaw.
It is the natural result of inner fragmentation: different parts of the psyche carrying different beliefs about safety, belonging, and vulnerability.

In shadow work, we see sabotage not as resistance to growth, but as protection from perceived danger.

The parts of ourselves that interfere with success, love, intimacy, abundance, or visibility are not malicious — they are wounded inner guardians acting based on outdated emotional information.

These parts hold tightly to the rules they once learned:

- "Don't trust too deeply."
- "Don't try too hard."
- "Don't reveal too much."
- "Don't get your hopes up."
- "Don't want more than you're allowed."
- "Don't become someone who could be hurt again."

When the psyche splits into fragments to survive emotional pain, each fragment develops its own strategy to prevent re-injury.

Those strategies — though logical at the time — become obstacles later in life.

WHY FRAGMENTATION OCCURS

Fragmentation forms in response to:

- abandonment or inconsistent love
- emotional neglect
- betrayal
- childhood shame
- humiliation
- chronic invalidation
- fear-based households
- conditional affection
- trauma that forced early emotional self-sufficiency

The psyche protects itself by tucking pieces away:

- the vulnerable one
- the intuitive one
- the passionate one
- the expressive one
- the one who needs affection
- the one who dreams boldly

When freedom, love, or authenticity led to pain, those parts were hidden for safety.

Reiki brings us back to them — not by force, but by presence.

HOW THESE PARTS SABOTAGE OUR PRESENT

The shadow does not sabotage because it fears failure. It sabotages because it fears what success might cost.

Growth requires vulnerability:

- more visibility
- deeper intimacy
- expanded trust
- emotional exposure
- greater responsibilities
- healthier boundaries

To the shadow, all of those are dangerous.

So sabotage becomes an instinctive defense against expansion.

It can look like:

- procrastination
- emotional shutdown
- isolating
- overthinking
- avoiding opportunity
- abandoning relationships prematurely
- choosing partners who cannot love deeply
- staying small
- self-doubt
- ignoring intuitions
- perfectionism
- dismissing desire
- collapsing into guilt or shame

These are not failures of willpower — they are psychic strategies.

They are inner children making adult decisions.

THE CONSCIOUS SELF VS. THE SHADOW SELF

When inner conflict arises, two parts speak simultaneously:

1. **The Conscious Self**
   wants to heal, grow, thrive, expand, connect.
2. **The Shadow Self**
   tries to prevent anything that resembles the original wound.

To the Conscious Self, love is a gift.
To the Shadow Self, love is a risk.

To the Conscious Self, success is fulfillment.
To the Shadow Self, success is exposure.

To the Conscious Self, expansion is destiny.
To the Shadow Self, expansion is vulnerability.

Reiki helps both parts sit at the same table.

It slows the emotional reflex long enough for truth to surface:
"I am sabotaging myself because this part of me is afraid."

That realization alone is a shift in consciousness.

SELF-SABOTAGE AS NERVOUS SYSTEM PROTECTION

Self-sabotage is the shadow's attempt to regulate the nervous system.

It does not want:

- activation
- unpredictability
- emotional uncertainty
- disappointment
- loss
- reminders of abandonment
- return of humiliation

So it shuts down possibility before possibility becomes risk.

It says:

- "If I never try, I cannot fail."
- "If I leave first, I cannot be left."
- "If I silence myself, I won't be judged."
- "If I stay small, I won't be seen."

These beliefs once made perfect sense.

Until Reiki begins to soften their grip.

FRAGMENTED PARTS IN THE CHAKRA SYSTEM

Many who struggle with sabotage carry fragmentation in several chakras:

- Root: mistrust, insecurity, need for rigid control
- Sacral: emotional suppression, fear of intimacy
- Solar Plexus: shame, rejection, unworthiness
- Heart: armored vulnerability, love as danger
- Throat: silence as self-protection
- Third Eye: doubt, self-mistrust, distorted perception
- Crown: spiritual disconnection, feeling unsupported by the Divine

Each of these chakras holds a piece of identity that learned:
"It is safer to disconnect from my fullness than to risk pain."

Reiki reunites those pieces with the whole self.

HOW REIKI BEGINS TO HEAL SABOTAGE PATTERNS

Reiki works on sabotage by:

- regulating emotional activation
- dissolving cellular memory of fear
- bringing unconscious narratives to awareness
- releasing energetic contraction
- softening defensive armor
- restoring intuition
- calming nervous system responses
- reconnecting inner parts to the present moment

As the body feels safer, the shadow loosens its guard.
No longer needing to prevent pain, it allows the self to expand again.

From this space:
dreams feel possible, intimacy feels breathable, connection feels safer, success feels deserved.

The fragmented self begins to reassemble.

REFRAMING THE INNER SABOTEUR

The greatest transformation occurs when the saboteur is no longer seen as an enemy.

Because once we understand its origin, we no longer feel hatred — we feel empathy.

Self-sabotage came from:

- a child trying to survive
- a heart trying not to break
- a nervous system trying to remain intact
- a soul that wasn't ready to risk vulnerability

That is not dysfunction.
That is intelligence.

The shadow deserves gratitude — not shame — for how it carried pain until the body was ready to heal.

Reiki invites a new inner dialogue:

- "Thank you for protecting me."
- "You can rest now."
- "I am strong enough to handle what you feared."

This is how fragmentation softens into wholeness.

THE BEGINNING OF RECONCILIATION

When Reiki touches the shadow, self-sabotage loses its power.

The subconscious begins to trust:

- emotional safety
- vulnerability
- belonging
- self-acceptance
- growth
- authentic expression

And slowly, what once felt threatening becomes natural.

Self-trust replaces fear.
Desire replaces avoidance.
Expansion replaces contraction.
Alignment replaces sabotage.

Every fragmented part that once pulled you away from love, connection, or success begins to return — not as a threat, but as a part of your inner council.

In Reiki-based shadow work, healing is not dominance but reunion.

A reunion with:

- power
- innocence
- intuition
- vulnerability
- purpose
- self-love

This is how sabotage ends:
not through discipline,
not through punishment,
but through remembering that every part of you wants to feel safe.

Reiki offers that safety.
And in its presence, inner conflict dissolves into wholeness.

Reiki Technique: Energy Integration for Inner Harmony

Reuniting the Fragmented Self Through Presence and Touch

Inner conflict arises when different parts of the self carry different emotional histories, beliefs, fears, and expectations. Some parts are bold and visionary. Others are terrified of loss. Some long for intimacy. Others brace for rejection.

Energy Integration is a Reiki technique designed to bring those inner parts back into relationship with each other. It creates an internal meeting place — a shared energetic field — where the body can experience unity rather than contradiction.

This technique doesn't force alignment.
It offers safety.
And safety allows natural coherence to return.

WHY INTEGRATION MATTERS

When the psyche fragments, the chakras often fragment with it:

- one chakra holding trauma
- another holding fear
- another holding shame
- another holding protection
- another holding spiritual withdrawal

Integration reconnects these parts to the same energetic network.

Through Reiki flow, the nervous system experiences:

- harmony instead of chaos

- inner conversation instead of suppression
- cooperation instead of resistance
- alignment instead of conflict

This is the moment shadow healing shifts from coping to transformation.

THE TECHNIQUE: ENERGY INTEGRATION FOR INNER HARMONY

You can perform this on yourself or with a client.
It works best with slow breath, gentle focus, and an open heart.

Move step by step — no rush.

1. Establish the Central Channel

Hands: one at the Crown, one at the Root (or held near).

This connects the upper spiritual centers with the lower emotional ones, inviting unity from the beginning.

Silently say:
"I allow all parts of myself to exist in the same space."

Imagine a soft current running down the spine.

This forms the central energetic corridor that the fragmented self can gather into.

2. Heart Bridge Position

Hands: one over the Heart, one over the Solar Plexus.

This placement is the foundation of integration work.

- The Heart: emotional truth, innocence, connection, compassion
- The Solar Plexus: identity, empowerment, self-image, shame release

Here, we are signaling the body:
"The version of me who hurts and the version of me who protects can meet here."

Visualize a subtle bridge of light between the two centers.

Let breath become slow and full.

3. Sacral Inclusion

Move the lower hand down to the Sacral Chakra.

Emotional fragmentation often begins here — where vulnerability, pleasure, authenticity, and emotional need were once denied.

Silently offer:
"I allow my emotions and intuition to be part of who I am."

Imagine all suppressed feelings being invited back into the present moment, one breath at a time.

4. Throat Honesty Alignment

Place one hand over the Throat, the other remaining at the Heart.

This integrates expression with feeling.

Many inner conflicts arise because one part wants honesty, while another fears the consequences.

Say:
"I allow truth and safety to coexist."

Feel the throat soften — even if no words are spoken.

The energetic message is enough.

5. Third Eye Reconnection

Move one hand to the Third Eye, the other still on the Heart.

Here, intuitive knowing and emotional truth meet.

Inner fragmentation often distorts perception:

- "I can't trust my feelings."
- "My intuition is dangerous."
- "I don't know who I am."

Reiki here clears those beliefs like fog.

Silently offer:
"I see myself clearly, with compassion, not judgment."

6. Crown Alignment

Place one hand lightly at the Crown, the other at the Solar Plexus or Heart.

Visualize the inner child, the protector, the critic, the dreamer, the wounded one, and the awakened self all sharing the same energetic field.

Say:
"I am one being, safe within myself."

Feel the alignment anchor.

7. Full Integration Sweep

Hover both hands a few inches above the body, moving slowly from Crown to Root.

Sweep lightly with intention:

- returning scattered parts
- dissolving inner conflict
- calling power home
- integrating wisdom
- softening defense

Imagine gathering threads of energy into the heart.

Slow, gentle, no force.

BREATH PATTERN FOR INTEGRATION

Breathe in through the nose:
receiving the exiled parts

Exhale through the mouth:
releasing resistance

Repeat:
Inhale: "I welcome my wholeness."
Exhale: "I release inner conflict."

This breath retrains the nervous system to respond to emotional activation with openness instead of fragmentation.

SIGNS THE TECHNIQUE IS WORKING

As integration begins, subtle shifts may appear:

- warmth in the heart
- softening of tension
- relief in the abdomen
- tingling along the spine
- quieter thoughts
- emotional clarity
- compassion toward the shadow
- sense of inner spaciousness

Sometimes tears rise.
Sometimes nothing is felt at all.

Both are integration.

Stillness is as valid as release.

THE CORE MESSAGE OF THE TECHNIQUE

Inner conflict is healed not by choosing one part over another, but by allowing all parts to sit at the same table.

When the shadow feels safe, it no longer needs to sabotage the present.

Reiki facilitates that safety by wrapping the fragmented self with neutrality, warmth, and presence.

A healed system whispers:

- "I am allowed to expand."
- "I am allowed to love."
- "I am allowed to receive."

- "I am allowed to be seen."
- "I am allowed to trust."

Integration is not the disappearance of shadow.

It is the realization that nothing within you is working against you.

Every part has been trying to protect you.

Reiki simply helps them remember that they no longer have to.

This is Inner Harmony:
the moment when all versions of you return to the heart and remember they are one.

Creating Energetic Alignment Between the Conscious and Unconscious Mind

Where Inner Decision and Hidden Belief Become One

True inner harmony requires more than awareness — it requires alignment.

Most people consciously desire growth, love, success, intimacy, creativity, purpose, or healing.
But beneath those desires lives an unconscious landscape shaped by past pain, survival instincts, and inherited beliefs.

If the conscious mind says,
"I want to thrive,"
but the unconscious mind still holds the memory,
"Thriving once led to hurt,"
then the body will unconsciously choose safety over expansion every time.

Alignment is the process of bringing conscious intention and unconscious protection into the same energetic truth.

Reiki becomes the translator between the two.

WHY CONSCIOUS DESIRE ISN'T ENOUGH

A person can:

- set goals
- speak affirmations
- visualize
- practice manifestation
- recite spiritual truths

Yet still fall into cycles that contradict their intentions.

This is not a failure of discipline or spiritual inadequacy.
It is the nervous system selecting safety based on old imprints rather than current reality.

The unconscious mind carries:

- stored memories
- met and unmet needs
- emotional programming
- identity conclusions
- beliefs shaped by childhood experiences
- cellular trauma
- unresolved grief
- generational patterning

These imprints live in the shadow and act beneath conscious choice.

Reiki reaches them through the energetic layers where those memories reside.

HOW ALIGNMENT IS CREATED THROUGH REIKI

Reiki quiets emotional activation long enough for both minds — conscious and unconscious — to “hear” each other.

During a session (or self-treatment):

- the nervous system shifts from survival mode into receptivity
- subtle memories surface
- suppressed emotion rises
- the body begins to recognize that the present is not the past

Once the body feels safe, the unconscious becomes available for dialogue.

This is where integration begins.

ALIGNMENT AS A THREE-PART ENERGETIC PROCESS

1. Awareness

The conscious mind witnesses the trigger, belief, emotion, or sabotaging pattern without judgment.

This step says:
"I see what I feel. I am willing to understand it."

Reiki slows internal turbulence enough for honesty.

2. Compassion

The unconscious part reveals itself without fear of rejection, punishment, or suppression.

This step says:
"Your pain was valid. You are not wrong for feeling this."

Reiki offers emotional safety, the ingredient needed for inner truths to surface.

3. Permission

The psyche reorganizes itself around updated truth.

This step says:
"It is safe to live differently now."

Reiki brings awareness into the energetic body, letting past beliefs loosen and dissolve.

When all three steps occur, alignment follows naturally.

ENERGETIC ALIGNMENT TECHNIQUE

This practice can be done during any Reiki session.

Step 1: Conscious Intention at the Solar Plexus

Place one hand over the Solar Plexus and ask:
"What do I consciously want for myself?"

Feel the answer in the body rather than thinking it.

Examples:

- "I want to trust."
- "I want to feel worthy."
- "I want to be loved."
- "I want to heal."

Let the intention settle like a seed.

Step 2: Dialogue with the Unconscious

Move the other hand to the Sacral or Heart.

Ask:
"What part of me is afraid of this?"

Let emotion, imagery, memory, sensation, or silence arise.

Instead of forcing answers, observe them.

Sometimes the unconscious speaks through:

- stomach tightness
- flashbacks
- sudden sadness
- numbness
- an inner voice
- a childlike feeling

Whatever comes is truth.

Step 3: Energetic Reconciliation

Bring both hands back to the Heart.

Say:
"I see both truths — the desire to grow and the instinct to protect."

Invite the unconscious to update its information:
"I am safe now. What hurt me then is not here today."

Let Reiki flow into both realities at once:
the longing and the fear.

This is how inner conflict dissolves — not through force, but through coexistence.

Step 4: Breath of Alignment

Inhale slowly into the chest,
exhale through the lower belly.

Breath connects the heart (emotional truth) and gut (instinctive memory).

Repeat silently:
"My heart and my history no longer need to fight."

This breath unwinds emotional reflexes stored in the unconscious.

Step 5: Crown & Root Integration

Hover one hand above the Crown and one near the Root.

This bridges the highest spiritual wisdom with the deepest survival imprint.

Say:
"All parts of me are allowed to choose the same direction."

Let Reiki form a current through the spine.

This is symbolic and energetic alignment:
the whole self pointing toward the same future.

SIGNS OF ALIGNMENT EMERGING

During or after this practice, people often notice:

- mental clarity
- reduced anxiety
- less resistance
- diminished sabotage impulses
- peace around goals
- ability to stay present with vulnerability
- a new sense of possibility
- "soft" courage instead of forceful will
- emotional honesty
- compassion for inner parts

And most commonly:
a deep inner knowing that growth no longer feels dangerous.

THE SUBTLE PSYCHOLOGY OF ALIGNMENT

When conscious and unconscious beliefs match, life feels less efforted.

Healing no longer feels like a battle.
Relationships feel less threatening.
Boundaries feel natural.
Success no longer triggers guilt or fear.
Love feels available.
Trust becomes breathable.

The shadow stops gripping the past, because it finally understands:
"The threat has passed."

And the conscious mind no longer has to fight for change, because the unconscious is no longer sabotaging it.

This is the moment when internal effort turns into internal harmony.

REIKI'S DEEPEST OFFER

At its core, Reiki offers the nervous system experiences that contradict the shadow's assumptions:

- "I am safe to feel."
- "I am safe to receive."
- "I am safe to expand."
- "I am safe to be seen."
- "I am safe to love."

When the body experiences safety, the unconscious updates its beliefs.

That is energetic alignment.

It is not done with pressure, demands, or self-discipline — but with patience, presence, breath, and unconditional compassion.

When the conscious desire
and the unconscious protection
finally recognize they want the same thing —
to be safe, whole, and free —

the psyche reorganizes itself.

And the shadow, once feared, becomes an ally.

Chapter 7:
Integrating Light
and Dark Energy
Through Reiki

Chapter 7: Integrating Light and Dark Energy Through Reiki

The Alchemical Union of Opposites

Light and shadow are not enemies — they are the two forces that shape wholeness.
One shows what has been healed.
The other shows what still seeks compassion.

In alchemy, transformation occurs when opposites are brought into relationship — fire and water, spirit and matter, ascent and descent. In the inner world, this union is found between our illuminated self and our shadowed self. Reiki becomes the vessel, the stabilizing element, and the energetic intelligence that allows that union to happen without force.

The true purpose of Reiki-based shadow work is not to purify the self of darkness, nor to bury the bright parts in guilt — but to help them speak to each other until they become one.

This is the alchemy of inner union.

THE MYTH OF PURITY

Many spiritual paths mistakenly chase perfection:

- "Only my light is worthy."
- "The darker parts must be erased."
- "I must transcend my humanity to be spiritual."

But nothing creates deeper fragmentation than trying to amputate one's own history.

The shadow is not darkness by moral definition; it is simply the parts of the psyche that were forced into silence or exile.

Reiki dissolves the need for purity by revealing a truth deeper than contrast:
both light and shadow are expressions of the same soul.

Light is consciousness in clarity.
Shadow is consciousness in waiting.

One is seen.
The other is asking to be seen.

ALCHEMY: WHEN OPPOSITES TRANSFORM EACH OTHER

In spiritual alchemy, opposite forces do not compete — they refine one another.

- Light without shadow becomes blind idealism.
- Shadow without light becomes despair.

But brought together through awareness, breath, and Reiki flow:

- light softens judgment

- shadow releases fear
- clarity meets vulnerability
- forgiveness rewrites narratives
- wisdom emerges from pain

This is the inner union that alchemists called the *coniunctio* — the sacred marriage.

In the modern healing landscape, Reiki provides the frequency that allows this union to unfold safely.

It holds the nervous system in neutrality so the shadow can be revealed without shame, and the light can remain stable without running from discomfort.

THE ENERGETICS OF UNION

Light and dark within the human psyche are energetic expressions of:

- joy and sorrow
- hope and grief
- courage and fear
- innocence and pain
- clarity and confusion
- love and protection

Where there is imbalance, the field cannot find harmony.

Reiki restores equilibrium by:

- releasing emotional charge
- softening the body's defense reflex
- dissolving identity distortions
- calming hypervigilance
- illuminating unconscious patterns
- infusing compassion where shame once lived

When energy flows through both the healed and wounded parts, neither dominates.
Both inform the other.

What emerges is not perfection, but wisdom.

THE SHADOW AS CATALYST

It is often the darkest moments that awaken spiritual insight: betrayals, heartbreak, illness, abandonment, grief, identity crisis.

These initiations activate spiritual sight because they strip away illusion.

The shadow says:
"Look where it hurts."

Reiki replies:
"You are not alone in the looking."

Together, they become the portal through which transformation occurs.

Light without descent lacks depth.
Shadow without illumination lacks direction.

Union is the ability to go inward with honesty and come outward with compassion.

REIKI AS THE MARRIAGE OF ABOVE AND BELOW

Every hand position in Reiki mirrors this inner union:

- Crown to Root
- Heart to Solar Plexus
- Sacral to Spine
- Third Eye to Heart
- Hands forming a circuit

Each placement says:
"What is unseen is allowed to meet what is known."

Reiki does not separate spiritual and human experience.
It weaves them.

It reminds us that intuition can coexist with reason, that vulnerability can coexist with strength, that grief can coexist with love.

Through Reiki, the duality within becomes dialogue rather than conflict.

WHEN LIGHT AND SHADOW EXCHANGE GIFTS

When the shadow meets the light:

- fear reveals courage
- shame unveils tenderness
- anger uncovers boundaries
- heartbreak awakens compassion
- grief deepens empathy
- insecurity teaches humility
- confusion expands curiosity

And when the light meets the shadow:

- clarity offers discernment
- awareness brings integration
- intuition restores trust
- compassion dissolves self-hatred
- honesty breaks illusion
- presence replaces avoidance

The union of both creates a deeper wholeness than either could hold alone.

THE MOMENT OF ALCHEMICAL SHIFT

There comes a quiet, unmistakable turning point in inner work:

It is when you look at the parts of yourself you once feared and realize you no longer wish to exile them.
When pain becomes teacher.
When vulnerability becomes power.
When the self you once judged becomes the self you now protect.

This is the moment alchemical union is achieved.

Not through achievement — but through surrender.

Reiki created the space.
Your awareness completed the act.

THE RESULT OF INTEGRATION

When light and shadow unite:

- the nervous system relaxes
- the body breathes differently
- emotional triggers lessen
- clarity arrives with softness
- empathy extends inward
- authenticity feels natural
- purpose feels embodied

You begin to live as someone no longer at war with themselves.

This is the deepest spiritual maturity:
To hold your history and your hopes in the same heart, without rejecting either.

THE TRUE UNION

Light without shadow is incomplete.
Shadow without light is directionless.

Together they form truth.

Shadow shows you where love is missing.
Light teaches you how to give that love.
Reiki allows both to exist without tension.

And from this union, the soul remembers itself.

For integration is not the removal of darkness —
but the recognition that nothing within you has ever been unholy.

Everything has been part of your becoming.

Understanding Wholeness as the Goal — Not Perfection

Perfection is a mask designed to protect us from shame, judgment, rejection, or vulnerability.
Wholeness, on the other hand, is a reclamation — an honest relationship with every part of our being.

In Reiki-based shadow work, the purpose is not to polish ourselves into purity or erase all emotional scars, but to live as a complete, integrated human who can hold complexity without collapsing into self-rejection.

Perfection demands a self that never falters.
Wholeness embraces a self that grows, learns, repairs, and returns.

THE ILLUSION OF "SPIRITUAL PERFECTION"

When healing is filtered through perfectionism, it becomes another layer of shadow judgment:

- "I shouldn't feel this."
- "I should be healed by now."
- "A spiritual person wouldn't struggle with this."
- "If I were aligned, I wouldn't be triggered."

These beliefs reinforce the same emotional exile that created the shadow in the first place.

They imply that some feelings are unacceptable — that grief, anger, insecurity, or fear signal spiritual failure rather than human truth.

But wholeness recognizes that every feeling is evidence of life force moving through us.

Reiki does not divide the self into "good" and "bad."
It moves through whatever is present, without hierarchy.

It teaches us that our humanity is not the obstacle to our growth — it is the vessel for it.

WHOLENESS IS INCOMPLETE WITHOUT THE SHADOW

To be whole means to make room for:

- the unhealed and the healing
- the strong and the scared
- the loving and the guarded
- the certain and the confused
- the peaceful and the angry

Shadow work reveals that all these aspects belong.

Pain is not proof of failure.
It is proof that the heart is still willing to feel.

Triggers are not regression.
They are openings — invitations to listen more deeply.

The shadow does not prevent wholeness.
It shows us where wholeness is still waiting to be restored.

WHY PERFECTION BLOCKS HEALING

Perfection creates pressure:

- emotional restriction
- shame around wounds
- fear of vulnerability
- avoidance of truth
- suppression of weakness

It traps energy, stiffens the body, and forces the unconscious deeper underground.

When the nervous system feels unsafe to feel, healing stalls.

Reiki works differently.

Its presence communicates:

- softness
- patience
- compassion
- neutrality
- unconditional permission

When the body senses that nothing within it is being judged, it naturally releases what is ready to move.

Wholeness emerges because nothing is forced to hide.

WHOLENESS ALLOWS THE SHADOW TO SPEAK WITHOUT FEAR

When wholeness — not perfection — is the aim:

- wounds can be acknowledged

- grief can be honored
- fear can be validated
- silence can be broken
- needs can be named
- truth can be spoken without apology

Reiki becomes the energetic field that holds all truths at once.

In that field, the shadow can tell its story:

- "I closed to protect you."
- "I doubted to spare you pain."
- "I hid because vulnerability once hurt."

This honesty is not weakness — it is integration.

It is how a fragmented self begins to reassemble.

WHOLENESS DOES NOT MEAN FREE OF PAIN

To be whole does not mean:

- never triggered
- never confused
- never afraid
- never grieving

It means that when those moments come, we do not abandon ourselves.

We stay.

We breathe.

We witness what rises.

And we offer compassion that used to be withheld.

That is the deepest freedom:
to feel without rejecting oneself.

THE ENERGETIC SIGNATURE OF WHOLENESS

When the body begins to live in wholeness, its field changes:

- the aura softens
- chakras move in sync
- the heart feels less armored
- intuition feels safer to trust
- relationships feel more honest
- internal dialogue becomes gentler
- nervous system regulation becomes easier

Energy no longer fractures into defense.
It circulates.

When the entire self is allowed to exist, the entire field can breathe.

REIKI AS THE EMBODIMENT OF WHOLENESS

Reiki already carries wholeness within it:

- it flows into every cell
- it enters every layer of the aura
- it touches pain without flinching
- it surrounds shame without judgment
- it reaches memory without retraumatization

When we allow that presence to permeate our inner world, we begin to treat ourselves the way Reiki treats us:
with neutrality, compassion, and spacious acceptance.

In this reflection, the psyche learns a new emotional truth:
"I do not need to be perfect to be worthy of love."

This is the release that changes everything.

WHOLENESS AS INTEGRATION, NOT ELIMINATION

The shadow does not disappear when healing is complete. Instead, it transforms into:

- instinct
- wisdom
- caution
- discernment
- emotional depth
- spiritual maturity
- empathy for others
- clarity about boundaries

What once defended becomes a guide.
What once hid becomes a voice.
What once blocked becomes an ally.

Perfection strips humanity.
Wholeness restores it.

THE FINAL TRUTH

The light within you is not diminished by your shadow.
The shadow is simply the part of you that needed tenderness to come forward.

When Reiki holds both simultaneously, opposites dissolve into unity.

Integration replaces division.

You stop trying to prove you are healed — and instead, you live as someone who no longer abandons themselves while healing.

This is the essence of wholeness:

the ability to hold every part of yourself with dignity, compassion, and belonging.

Perfection isolates.
Wholeness liberates.

And in that liberation, the soul remembers who it truly is.

Reiki Visualization: The Inner Temple of Light and Shadow

A Guided Journey into the Sacred Center of Integration

This visualization is designed to help you witness light and shadow as two expressions of the same soul — not opposing forces, but complementary truths.
Move slowly. Allow every sensation, image, or emotion to arise without judgment.

If possible, place one hand over the Heart and one over the Solar Plexus as you begin, letting Reiki flow.

ENTERING THE INNER TEMPLE

Breathe deeply.
Let your awareness travel inward, past thought and memory, past identity and story, into the quiet field beneath it all.

Imagine walking a path that leads into your own inner world.
The air is calm.
The space feels familiar — ancient, yet undeniably yours.

Ahead, you see a doorway.
It may appear as stone, wood, light, crystal, or simple presence.

Beyond this doorway lies the Temple of Light and Shadow — the inner sanctuary where every part of you is allowed to exist.

When you feel ready, step through.

Inside, the temple glows with a gentle, ambient radiance. Some areas are illuminated, others cast in soft shadow.

Both feel safe.

Both feel sacred.

Notice the architecture:

- curved archways
- quiet chambers
- reflective surfaces
- flowing light
- walls that seem to breathe
- or open space without boundaries

Everything here symbolizes the psyche — the known and the hidden, the conscious and the unconscious.

Allow Reiki to fill the space like air.

In one part of the temple, shadow gathers — not as darkness to fear, but as the unseen aspects of your inner world.

Your shadow may appear as:

- a younger self
- a figure cloaked in softness
- a symbolic shape
- a memory
- a familiar presence
- a feeling or sensation

It holds vulnerability, truth, emotional weight, survival instincts, and self-protection.

Approach gently.

Place a hand over the heart and silently offer:
"I see you. I am ready to listen."

Let Reiki flow from your palms into this presence.
No fixing.
No forcing.
Only openness.

Notice what emotions, sensations, or thoughts arise.

In another part of the temple, light gathers — radiant, calm, and clarifying.

It may appear as:

- a glowing form
- a luminous version of yourself
- an inner guide
- a pillar of energy
- a warm presence

It holds compassion, intuition, clarity, higher awareness, forgiveness, love, and spiritual insight.

Let your gaze rest on this light.

Place your other hand at the Crown or Third Eye and say:
"I welcome the wisdom within me."

Feel Reiki infusing this presence.

Now imagine both embodiments — Light and Shadow — slowly approaching one another.

There is no fear.
Only recognition.

The Shadow steps forward carrying:

- memories
- wounds
- emotions
- lessons
- resilience

The Light steps forward carrying:

- compassion
- clarity
- healing
- patience
- unconditional acceptance

They do not merge by force.
They simply stand before each other, sharing space.

Whisper inwardly:
"What is hidden and what is known now meet without conflict."

Let Reiki form a bridge between them — a soft glow that connects their shared essence.

Observe the silent dialogue between them:

- The Shadow offering truth that once felt too heavy to bear.
- The Light offering warmth that once felt too vulnerable to receive.

Let the exchange unfold naturally:
wisdom passing in both directions.

Light does not try to "fix."
Shadow does not try to conceal.

They recognize they have always been one being — separated only by fear and misunderstanding.

Bring both hands to the Heart Chakra.

Invite Light and Shadow to rest there.

See them as one presence now:
the you that survived
and the you that aspires.

Say inwardly:
"I honor every part of who I have been and who I am becoming."

Feel the heart expand —
warmth, softness, breath, or simple stillness.

The reunion is quiet, but profound.

It is the nervous system allowing unity.

Visualize Reiki filling the temple, saturating every chamber — from the brightest corners to the softest shadows.

Let the energy circulate through:

- memory
- identity
- intuition
- vulnerability
- belief
- emotion

Everything belongs.
Nothing is exiled.

Whisper:
"I am whole. Nothing within me is against me."

Let the aura absorb this truth.

Gently step back toward the doorway.

Before crossing through, look once more at the temple —
its light,
its shadows,
its stillness.

Know that it remains within you always.

Whisper goodbye not as separation, but as acknowledgment:
"I will return."

Step through the doorway.
Feel awareness travel back into the body:

- breath
- heartbeat
- weight and posture
- hands
- feet

Inhale deeply.
Exhale fully.

When ready, open the eyes.

UNDERSTANDING THE VISION

This visualization is not symbolic fiction —
it mirrors the way the psyche naturally organizes itself when given energetic safety.

Light is clarity.
Shadow is protection.
Reiki is the mediator.

And when all three coexist without conflict, integration is inevitable.

This temple is your inner world in harmony:

- where wounds meet wisdom
- where innocence meets insight
- where the human self meets the spiritual self
- where the past is welcomed and not denied

Shadow and light are no longer opposing forces —
they are companions walking the same path.

This is the deepest work:
to see yourself without division.

To know that wholeness has always been yours.

Reiki simply helped you remember.

CHAPTER 8:
THE ONGOING
JOURNEY OF SOUL
INTEGRATION

Chapter 8: The Ongoing Journey of Soul Integration

Continuing the Work After a Major Breakthrough

Shadow healing often brings moments of profound clarity — an old belief dissolves, a trigger softens, a memory releases, intuition opens, or self-compassion awakens for the first time.

These breakthroughs are sacred.

They mark the moment when a part of the psyche finally feels safe enough to be seen.

But they are not the ending.

They are the doorway.

Integration is not achieved in a single moment of awakening. It is cultivated through repetition, presence, and continued relationship with the inner world.

Shadow work asks us to show up again and again — not because we are broken, but because healing is a living process that unfolds with time.

The breakthrough is the opening.
What comes next is embodiment.

THE QUIET AFTER THE REVELATION

After a powerful emotional release or energetic shift, many people expect permanent ease — never feeling triggered, never doubting, never grieving again.

But the nervous system does not rewrite a lifetime of survival patterns in one moment.
It needs repetition, reassurance, and continued safety to complete its transformation.

Breakthroughs loosen the roots.
Continued presence allows them to lift.

It is normal — and even healthy — for emotions to resurface after release.
Not as regressions, but as echoes asking to be met with the new awareness you have gained.

Your task is no longer to fight them, but to meet them with compassion.

That is the continuation of the work.

THE SPIRAL PATH OF INTEGRATION

Healing does not move in a straight line.

It spirals:

- returning us to old memories
- revisiting wounds from deeper angles
- showing familiar patterns in new light
- offering compassion where shame once lived

Each time we circle back, we arrive with more clarity, strength, tenderness, and self-trust.

What once triggered collapse may now only stir curiosity. What once felt unbearable may feel manageable, even meaningful.

This is progress — even if the emotion itself looks similar on the surface.

The shift is in how you meet it.

WHY THE SHADOW NEEDS ONGOING RELATIONSHIP

The shadow carries emotional truths about moments when the self was not safe, seen, understood, or protected.

It needs:

- consistency
- presence
- gentleness
- space
- patience

Just as a child who has been hurt learns to trust slowly, the shadow learns to relax over time.

When you return to it repeatedly — not in fear, but in invitation — the shadow begins to believe that hiding is no longer necessary.

This is why the work continues after breakthroughs:
you are establishing a new internal bond based on compassion rather than suppression.

Reiki helps nurture that bond every time it flows through the body.

BREAKTHROUGHS AS NEW BEGINNINGS

After each energetic opening, it is helpful to ask:

- "What truth is revealed now that I can see more clearly?"
- "How can I live differently with this insight?"
- "What behaviors or boundaries align with this new awareness?"
- "What gentleness can I offer myself while this settles?"

Breakthroughs give us information.
Integration gives us embodiment.

Reiki bridges the two.

It holds the nervous system steady while your emotional landscape reorganizes itself around truth.

PRACTICES THAT SUSTAIN INTEGRATION

1. Daily Reiki Check-Ins

Even 5 minutes of hand placement on the Heart, Solar Plexus, or Sacral chakra reinforces emotional safety.

It tells the subconscious:
"I am still here with you."

2. Gentle Journaling

Not to analyze, but to witness:

- changes
- insights
- new emotional responses
- softening triggers
- compassionate self-talk

3. Breathwork

Slow breath helps the body believe what the mind has learned.

4. Honoring Grief

Sometimes breakthroughs reveal grief that was never moved through.
Allow tears, silence, rest.

5. Revisiting Old Memories with Compassion

Return to the past through the lens of who you are now — not who you were then.

6. Chakra Reflection

Notice which centers feel open, which feel tight, and place hands accordingly.

7. Sharing Truth Safely

Speak feelings aloud with someone you trust.
Voice anchors transformation into the physical world.

8. Saying No Where You Once Abandoned Yourself

Boundaries are integration in motion.

ALLOWING YOURSELF TIME

Some wounds release quickly.
Others unwind layer by layer.

If an emotion resurfaces after a breakthrough, it does not mean you failed — it means your body trusts you enough to reveal another piece of the truth.

The deeper the original wound, the more patience required.

Reiki teaches us that healing is not rushed — it unfolds naturally with breath, presence, and compassion.

LIVING WITH THE INTEGRATED SELF

Integration expresses itself in subtle changes:

- defensiveness softens
- reactions become responses
- attachments loosen
- self-silencing fades
- boundaries feel healthy
- vulnerability feels less threatening
- intuition feels clearer
- inner dialogue becomes kinder

You may still feel emotion, but you no longer fear it.
You may still have needs, but you no longer shame them.
You may still encounter triggers, but you meet them as teachers.

Shadow becomes wisdom.
Light becomes compassion.
And the self becomes unified.

THE GIFT OF CONTINUAL INTEGRATION

The journey never ends — not because we are incomplete, but because wholeness continues to deepen.

Every breakthrough refines:

- who you are
- how you love
- how you trust
- how you stand in your truth
- how you hold your own humanity

Each layer brings more tenderness.
Each descent brings more awareness.
Each integration reveals more strength.

The goal is not to reach a perfect state.
The goal is to live as someone who never abandons their inner world again.

Reiki is the reminder, every time your hands touch your body:
"I stay with myself."

That is lifelong integration.

How to Know When You've Reached a New Level of Integration

Integration doesn't announce itself with fireworks.
It isn't dramatic.
It rarely arrives in a single moment of revelation.

Instead, it reveals itself quietly — in small inner shifts that signal the nervous system no longer feels threatened by vulnerability, truth, or emotional honesty.

Integration is recognized by the *way you feel when old patterns arise.*
Not whether they appear, but how your relationship to them changes.

Below are the most common indicators that shadow work and Reiki have brought you into a new layer of wholeness.

1. Emotional Triggers Feel Less Dangerous

You no longer panic when you feel:

- activation
- discomfort
- grief
- insecurity
- fear
- old memories rising

Instead of collapsing inward or fighting the sensation, you allow it to unfold.

Your inner dialogue shifts from:

- "Something is wrong,"
  to
- "Something is speaking."

You can sit with the activation long enough to hear it.

That alone is profound integration.

2. Reaction Turns Into Curiosity

Where you once felt the need to defend, withdraw, or attack, you now feel drawn to understand:

- "What is this showing me?"
- "Where did this begin?"
- "What part of me feels unsafe?"

Triggers become portals instead of traps.

Curiosity replaces self-judgment.

3. You Speak to Yourself with Love Instead of Condemnation

Self-talk softens.

You no longer call yourself weak, broken, dramatic, or difficult.

The inner voice becomes:

- tender
- validating
- patient
- curious
- protective

You stop punishing yourself for feeling pain.

Compassion has taken root.

4. Old Wounds Rise Without Overpowering the Present

Memories lose their sharp edge.

Instead of re-living them, you observe them from a grounded distance — not dissociated, but supported.

Your body no longer mistakes the past for the present.

This is trauma resolving at the nervous system level.

5. You No Longer Fear Your Own Depth

Where strong emotion once felt threatening, you now feel capable of holding it.

You trust yourself to:

- process
- breathe
- witness
- soothe
- wait

Your emotional range becomes proof of vitality, not danger.

You feel deep — but not fragile.

6. Authenticity Comes More Naturally

You notice yourself:

- expressing truth with less fear
- setting boundaries without guilt
- saying no without panic
- admitting needs without shame
- sharing vulnerability without collapse

You begin to feel safe being seen.

Not for a polished version of you —
but for the whole truth.

7. Relationship Dynamics Shift

Instead of repeating old injury cycles, you:

- notice red flags sooner
- choose partners who can meet you
- stop chasing love that requires self-abandonment
- communicate openly
- walk away from what harms you
- allow intimacy that once terrified you

Connection becomes a place of breath, not bracing.

8. You Release Identities Rooted in Wounds

You no longer define yourself by:

- betrayal
- abandonment
- unworthiness
- exclusion

- guilt
- perfectionism

Those narratives may still arise, but they no longer feel like truth.

You sense the self beneath the wound.

9. You Feel More Present in Your Body

Integration shows up as:

- unclenched muscles
- open chest
- deeper breath
- warmth in the abdomen
- fewer stress reflexes
- steadier heartbeat during vulnerability

Your body trusts you again — or perhaps for the first time.

10. Safety Comes From Within, Not From Control

You stop trying to control the external world to prevent emotional harm.

Instead, you feel safe because you know you won't abandon yourself if pain arises.

This is the breakthrough that turns into embodiment:
the self becomes the source of safety.

11. You Experience Quiet Confidence

Not arrogance.
Not performance.
Not spiritual ego.

Just a grounded knowing:

- "I can handle what comes."
- "I do not need to hide."
- "I can face myself."

Shame loses its authority.

Fear loses its center of power.

12. You Forgive Yourself for What You Didn't Know Before

Instead of resenting past versions of yourself, you thank them.

You recognize they were doing what they could with the emotional tools they had.

This is emotional adulthood — and the shadow feels safe in its presence.

13. You No Longer See Darkness as an Enemy

You stop dividing your inner world into:

- light vs. shadow
- healed vs. unhealed
- worthy vs. unworthy

Instead, you see all experiences as information, growth, and evolution.

And you meet the shadow with reverence.

Integration becomes a form of sacred relationship.

14. Reiki Feels Like Coming Home

Instead of "using Reiki to manage pain," you experience Reiki as an extension of who you are:

- gentle
- aware
- compassionate
- grounded
- receptive

Energy flows more easily, because there is no longer internal resistance.

The field feels coherent.

THE CORE SIGN IS SIMPLE

You know you have reached a deeper level of integration when you no longer abandon yourself — emotionally, energetically, or spiritually — when discomfort arises.

You stay.

You breathe.

You listen.

You offer compassion instead of exile.

This consistency is the true marker of inner evolution.

Integration is not perfection.
It is loyalty to your own wholeness.

And once that loyalty takes root, nothing inside you feels foreign anymore.

The shadow becomes an honored guest.
The past becomes a teacher.
And Reiki becomes a language of truth.

This is how you know:

Your healing is no longer something you "do."
It has become the way you live.

How to Support Others in Their Own Shadow Healing

Supporting someone through shadow work is a sacred responsibility.
Whether you are a Reiki practitioner, a teacher, a guide, or simply a compassionate presence in someone's life, the way you hold space matters more than anything you say or do.

Shadow work is vulnerable terrain.
It takes people down to the roots of identity, memory, defense, survival, and emotional truth.
To walk beside someone in that space requires humility, patience, and a deep respect for the sacred intelligence of the human psyche.

Below are the foundational principles of supporting others in their journey.

1. Never Force Revelation

The shadow reveals itself only when it feels safe.

Do not push:

- confessions
- emotional exposure
- trauma stories
- catharsis
- forgiveness
- breakthroughs

Your job is not to dig.

Your job is to hold presence.

Let their nervous system decide the pace.

Shadow work blooms through permission — not pressure.

2. Create an Energetic Field of Neutrality

When offering Reiki:

- release personal agendas
- silence internal judgments
- soften assumptions
- drop expectations of outcomes

The shadow retreats from anything that feels like evaluation.

Neutrality tells the wounded self:
"You can be exactly as you are here."

This alone can unlock years of tightness, suppression, and guardedness.

3. Listen More Than You Interpret

People do not need analysis — they need space to hear themselves.

Ask gentle questions:

- "Where do you feel that in your body?"
- "What emotion is underneath the surface?"
- "What does that part of you believe?"

Allow their inner wisdom to lead.

You are not the authority — you are the witness.

4. Do Not Rescue Them From Their Feelings

Sadness, anger, shame, grief, fear — these are not failures.

They are messengers.

If someone cries, shakes, or becomes emotional:

- ground your breath
- let Reiki flow
- remain steady

Trying to soothe too quickly can imply:
"This feeling shouldn't exist."

Instead, communicate energetically:
"I trust your capacity to feel this."

5. Protect Their Autonomy

Do not tell someone:

- what their shadow is
- who they should forgive
- what meaning a memory holds
- what lesson they "need" to learn
- when something is "complete"

Interpretation can re-traumatize — it replaces their voice with yours.

Empower them to find their own understanding.

The shadow trusts only when the person remains in authorship of their story.

6. Keep Their Pain Confidential

Shadow work requires vulnerability.
Respect privacy like a sacred vow.

Energetic trust collapses the moment someone fears you may expose their truth.

Hold their story in silence.

Always.

7. Validate Their Experience Without Amplifying It

If they feel:

- betrayed
- unlovable
- ashamed
- abandoned
- broken
- not enough

Do not dispute the feeling.

Say:
"It makes sense that you feel that."
"That part of you deserves to be heard."

Validation turns pain into presence.

It tells the shadow:
"I am safe to exist."

8. Keep Your Nervous System Steady

Your calm becomes their anchor.

If you panic, rush, over-explain, or tighten, their body will read: "I am too much."

Instead:

- slow your breath
- soften your gaze
- relax your shoulders
- stay grounded

Your coherence becomes medicine.

9. Offer Reiki as Gentle Illumination, Not Fixing

Let Reiki:

- soften tightness
- warm emotional numbness
- dissolve fear
- open breath
- stabilize the heart

But never treat Reiki as a tool of correction.

You are not "clearing" someone's shadow.

You are helping them hold it with compassion.

Reiki is an invitation — not a cure.

10. Trust Their Timing

Shadow work unfolds in layers:

- insights rise slowly
- memories surface when ready
- emotional skills build over time
- forgiveness blooms organically

If someone revisits a wound again and again, do not rush them forward.

They are circling the spiral — each time from a higher level of consciousness.

11. Normalize the Waves

Remind them:

- healing is not linear
- pain does not mean failure
- numbness is not regression
- closure takes time
- vulnerability is strength

Unlearning self-rejection is a long process.

Be the voice that honors their progress — especially when they can't see it.

12. Do Not Become Their Source of Safety

Your presence should help them feel safe with themselves — not dependent on you.

Encourage:

- inner resources
- self-soothing
- personal agency
- emotional resilience
- grounding techniques
- self-Reiki practices

Empowerment, not attachment, is the true goal.

13. Bow to Their Inner Wisdom

Even in their confusion, a person's psyche knows what it's doing.

It protects until it's safe.
It reveals when ready.
It integrates when supported.

Assume the intelligence of the shadow.
Never treat anyone as fragile or incapable.

Your faith becomes their mirror.

14. Know When to Step Aside

If someone's shadow holds:

- deep trauma
- suicidal ideation
- severe anxiety
- self-harm
- dissociation
- medical concerns

Encourage professional therapy or trauma-informed care.

This is not abandonment.
It is integrity.

Reiki can hold — but some wounds need additional support.

15. See Their Light and Shadow as One

Do not pedestal their "light" nor fear their "darkness."

They are both reflections of the same soul:

- one learns
- one protects
- one remembers

When you hold both with equal respect, the person learns to do the same.

And that is the heart of shadow integration.

THE GREATEST GIFT YOU CAN OFFER

In shadow work, you are not a healer of wounds.
You are a companion to truth.

You sit beside someone as they remember:

- their innocence
- their inner strength
- their capacity to feel
- their worth
- their wisdom
- their belonging

The shadow relaxes where it is welcomed.
And Reiki becomes the gentle bridge that says:

"You do not need to hide here.
You are safe to be whole."

That is how we support others —
not by leading them out of their darkness,
but by holding the lantern while they learn to walk with it.

BONUSES

Bonus 1: Reiki Symbols for Shadow Work

The Reiki symbols act as energetic keys — consciousness triggers that awaken deeper resonance within the body, mind, and soul.
They do not control energy, force change, or override emotional truth.
Instead, they open inner channels, soften resistance, and illuminate suppressed wounds so they can be met with compassion.

When used with shadow work, the symbols create an energetic field that feels safe enough for honesty, grief, revelation, and release.

Below are the three primary symbols most supportive during shadow integration.

GUIDELINES FOR USING THE SYMBOLS IN SHADOW WORK

1. Use Them With Humility

Symbols are not commands.
They are doorways.
Let them work gently, not forcefully.

2. Do Not Rush Emotional Release

Tears, numbness, silence, shaking, or stillness are all valid.

3. Let the Nervous System Lead

If the body tightens, pause and ground before continuing.

4. Use Only When Invited by the Inner Self

Never impose them out of fear or desperation.
Call them with reverence.

5. Trust the Shadow's Timing

Emotional revelation happens when the psyche feels safe — not when we demand insight.

Hon Sha Ze Sho Nen

The Bridge Through Time and Trauma

Primary Uses in Shadow Work:

- working with past emotional wounds
- childhood imprints
- inherited trauma
- memories that replay as triggers
- beliefs formed from early pain
- karmic patterns
- soul fractures caused by rejection or fear

The essence of Hon Sha Ze Sho Nen is *connection* — specifically, the restoration of wholeness across all timelines.

Shadow work often touches memories where the self split in order to survive:

- pretending
- silencing
- shrinking
- numbing
- abandoning inner truth

This symbol creates a compassionate bridge between your present self and the younger parts who still carry emotional shock, shame, confusion, or longing.

When you activate it during self-Reiki:

1. place hands over the Heart or Solar Plexus
2. breathe slowly into the memory, sensation, or emotion that is rising
3. call the symbol mentally or aloud
4. imagine a thread of light traveling into the moment where the wound began

Let the symbol hold space for that version of you.
Do not force resolution.
Do not chase forgiveness.
Simply be a loving witness.

Hon Sha Ze Sho Nen reminds the inner child:
"You are remembered. You are not alone anymore."

That alone begins repair.

Sei He Ki

The Balancer of Emotion and Mind

Primary Uses in Shadow Work:

- emotional triggers
- self-rejection
- guilt
- shame
- grief
- anxiety
- internal conflict
- sabotaging thoughts
- trauma symptoms stored in the body

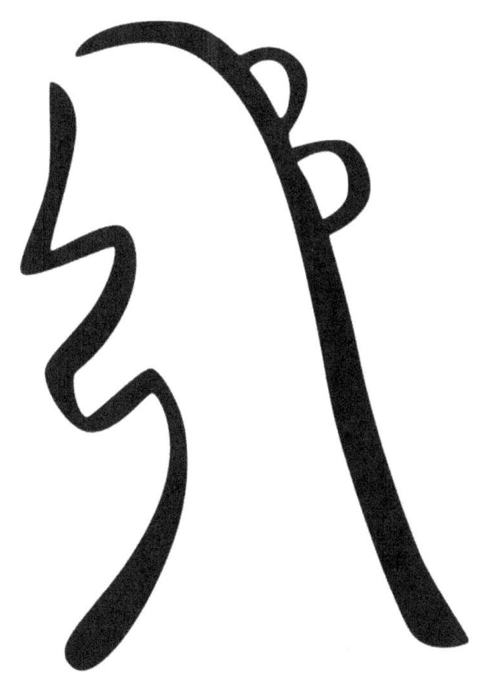

Sei He Ki harmonizes the emotional body with the mental field. It dissolves the energetic walls built from:

- rejection
- abandonment
- humiliation
- betrayal
- conditional love

Where the shadow clings tightly to wounded identity, Sei He Ki unravels the emotional charge that keeps those memories frozen in time.

It is a symbol of deep permission.

It whispers:
"Your feelings are safe to be felt."

During shadow sessions:

- draw or visualize Sei He Ki over the Heart
- hold Reiki over the Solar Plexus
- breathe into the sensations that rise

Instead of trying to "fix" emotion, allow the symbol to soften it.
Shame turns to acknowledgement.
Anger becomes honesty.
Sadness becomes truth.
Fear becomes vulnerability.

Sei He Ki doesn't erase emotion —
it helps the nervous system loosen its grip long enough for compassion to take its place.

Dai Ko Myo

The Light of Spiritual Integration

Primary Uses in Shadow Work:

- spiritual fragmentation
- loss of identity
- self-condemnation
- deep existential wounds
- inner conflict connected to belief
- unworthiness
- disconnection from intuition, divinity, or purpose

Dai Ko Myo is the master frequency of remembrance.
It illuminates the truth that exists beneath every trauma, shadow, and survival pattern:
You are inherently whole.

In darkness, we forget who we are.
We mistake emotional scars for spiritual identity.
We believe we are unworthy because pain convinced us so.

Dai Ko Myo restores spiritual memory.

It does not force enlightenment —
it opens the inner chamber where light has been waiting.

When held during meditation or hands-on healing:

- place hands over Crown and Third Eye
- breathe slowly
- visualize a soft radiance glowing from within
- allow it to spread down the spine and into the Heart

This symbol reminds the psyche that the shadow is not an enemy or flaw —
it is the voice of a younger self still longing for acceptance.

Dai Ko Myo is most powerful not when used to "banish the dark,"
but when used to embrace it.

It is the light that joins hands with the shadow and says:
"You belong to me."

From that union, spiritual coherence emerges.

WHEN USED TOGETHER

These symbols support three layers of shadow healing:

Hon Sha Ze Sho Nen
heals the origin of the wound

Sei He Ki
balances its emotional charge

Dai Ko Myo
integrates it into spiritual wholeness

Where trauma once fragmented,
Reiki restores coherence.

Where the psyche once shut down,
Reiki invites presence.

Where the inner child once hid,
Reiki whispers:
"You are safe now."

The symbols do not cure the shadow —
they comfort it.

They do not erase memory —
they hold it in love.

They do not demand change —
they reveal truth.

And in that gentle revelation, shadow begins to soften, open, and finally return home.

Bonus 2: Guided Meditations & Scripts

These meditations are designed to facilitate deep emotional release, inner re-alignment, and gentle shadow integration. They may be practiced silently, read aloud, or recorded in your own voice.

Before beginning any of them:

- Invite Reiki to flow
- Slow your breath
- Keep your nervous system relaxed
- Allow emotion without resistance

Use hands on the body when prompted or wherever you are intuitively guided.

1. Shadow Integration Meditation

Bringing Compassion to the Forgotten Parts of Self

Opening the Field

Sit comfortably with your spine upright.
Place one hand on your Heart Chakra, and the other on your Solar Plexus.

Inhale, and say inwardly:
"Reiki now flows through every layer of my being."

Exhale, and allow your awareness to sink inward — beneath thoughts, into presence.

Meeting the Shadow

Visualize a path forming in front of you — wide enough to walk, leading into an inner landscape.

Notice the colors, the ground beneath your feet, the air, the sky.

Ahead, a figure waits.

This is your shadow:

- the emotions you swallowed
- the memories you minimized
- the parts you deemed unlovable
- the versions of yourself that survived what you couldn't name

Approach without urgency.

When you are close, speak inwardly:
"I am ready to see you with compassion."

Observe what arises:

- an image
- a sensation
- a memory
- a feeling
- words

There is no right form.

Listening to Truth

Ask gently:
"What have you been holding for me?"

Let the answer form slowly.
It may come as:

- emotion
- silence
- grief
- clarity
- confusion
- warmth

Both answers and silence are valid.

If discomfort arises, soften your breath and allow Reiki to expand through your chest.

Offering Acceptance

Place both hands now over the Heart.

Say inwardly or aloud:
"You no longer need to hide.
You are safe with me.
I honor your pain.
I honor your protection.
Thank you for carrying what I could not face."

Let Reiki surround the shadow with warmth.

No erasing.
No forcing.
Only presence.

Integration

Invite the shadow closer — not to be absorbed or dissolved, but to stand beside you.

Whisper:
"I will walk with you."

Feel the body soften.

When ready, visualize the shadow stepping into your heart-center — not merging, but resting there as a welcomed truth of who you are.

Inhale deeply.
Exhale fully.

Open the eyes when ready.

2. Cord Release with Forgiveness

Letting Go of Emotional Attachments While Honoring the Lesson

Use this meditation when the shadow reveals:

- a wound caused by another
- betrayal
- abandonment
- criticism
- guilt
- memories that bind the heart

Forgiveness here is not absolution of the past —
but release of emotional charge so the self can breathe again.

Beginning the Work

Place hands over the Heart and Solar Plexus.
Call in Reiki with intention.

Bring to mind the person, memory, situation, or belief that holds emotional tension.

Observe any sensation:

- heaviness
- ache
- tightness
- numbness

No analysis — only honesty.

Energetic Cord Awareness

Visualize a cord connecting you to this emotional bond:
It may appear as:

- a rope
- a thread
- vines
- barbed wire
- a beam of light
- mist
- pure feeling

Its texture reveals the emotional quality — not moral judgement.

Touch the cord with your inner awareness and say:
"I see the bond between us."

Seeing the Lesson

Ask silently:
"What have you been trying to teach me?"

Let truth emerge.

Common themes:

- boundaries
- self-worth
- courage
- voice
- self-protection
- discernment
- resilience
- honesty

Reiki holds the heart open while the mind witnesses.

Forgiveness as Release

With hands on the Heart, say inwardly:
"I release the emotional weight of this bond."
"I forgive what I needed to hold in order to survive."
"I keep the wisdom. I release the pain."

If forgiveness toward a person is not accessible:
Shift it inward:
"I forgive myself for carrying this longer than I needed to."

That alone breaks karmic repetition.

Realeasing the Cord

Visualize Reiki gathering at your hands.
Draw Hon Sha Ze Sho Nen or Sei He Ki mentally if trained.

Imagine the cord dissolving, unraveling, melting — not severed in violence but undone with clarity.

Say:
"We are no longer bound in suffering."

The memory remains.
The lesson remains.
But the emotional weight lifts.

Breathe.

Completion

Place hands on the Sacral or Solar Plexus.

Whisper:
"I release with love.
I walk forward with freedom."

Open your eyes when ready.

3. Chakra Balancing for Inner Peace

Reiki Alignment for Emotional and Energetic Harmony

This meditation is for grounding, regulation, and emotional stability.
It can be used after deep shadow work, during nervous system activation, or simply as energetic maintenance.

Opening

Sit or lie comfortably.

Place both hands anywhere on the body where they naturally settle and call in Reiki.

Say inwardly:
"My energy returns to balance and harmony."

Root Chakra

Bring awareness to the base of the spine.

Visualize a red light glowing steadily.

Say:
"I am safe in my body."
"I belong in the world."

Let Reiki ground and stabilize you.

Sacral Chakra

Move awareness to the lower abdomen.

Visualize warm orange light.

Say:
"My feelings are honored."
"I deserve joy, expression, and intimacy."

Reiki melts emotional rigidity and awakens softness.

Solar Plexus Chakra

Shift to the space above the navel.

Visualize radiant yellow.

Say:
"I claim my inner power."
"I act with confidence, clarity, and self-respect."

Reiki strengthens identity and dissolves self-rejection.

Heart Chakra

Bring awareness to the chest.

Visualize soft green or pink light.

Say:
"I am worthy of love, compassion, and connection."

Let Reiki relax the heart and release defense.

Throat Chakra

Visualize blue light at the throat.

Say:
"My voice matters.
I speak truth without fear."

Reiki opens expression and dissolves silence rooted in shame.

Third Eye Chakra

Visualize indigo light between the brows.

Say:
"I trust my inner wisdom."
"I see clearly within myself."

Reiki quiets the mind, sharpens intuition, and softens doubt.

Crown Chakra

Visualize violet or white light above the head.

Say:
"I am supported by the universe."
"I remember who I am."

Reiki reconnects with faith, higher truth, and spiritual coherence.

FULL AURA INTEGRATION

Now imagine all seven chakras shining simultaneously:

- grounded
- open
- aligned

Energy flows smoothly from root to crown.

Place hands on the Heart and breathe deeply.

Whisper:
"I allow peace to settle within me."

Let stillness be the closing.

Open the eyes when ready.

✦ FINAL NOTE

These meditations are internal sanctuaries.

They do not chase release, force transformation, or impose interpretation.

They simply clear space within the energetic body so the shadow can:

- reveal
- integrate
- soften
- heal

Reiki offers light. You offer presence. And together, they become wholeness.

Bonus 3: Journal Section for Shadow Healing

Shadow work becomes truly transformative when processed through reflection.
Writing creates spaciousness between experience and understanding — allowing insight, emotional clarity, and integration to take root.

This journal section is designed to:

- deepen your inner dialogue
- track emotional shifts over time
- witness the shadow with compassion
- ground breakthroughs
- help you recognize patterns gently

Move through these pages at your own pace.
Some prompts may need a day.
Others may need a week.

Let intuition lead the timeline.

A. 30 Days of Shadow Work Prompts

Gentle, Progressive, Trauma-Safe

Each prompt invites awareness, not confrontation.
If strong emotion rises, pause and place your hands over your Heart or Solar Plexus, allowing Reiki to flow before continuing.

WEEK ONE — MEETING THE SHADOW

Focus: recognition, permission, honesty

1. What emotion or pattern shows up most often when I feel unsafe or triggered?
2. What age or version of me first learned that this emotion needed to be hidden?
3. If that younger self could speak freely, what would they say about what happened?
4. What part of me still believes that vulnerability is dangerous?
5. When have I abandoned myself emotionally to avoid conflict or rejection?
6. What version of me appears when I feel insecure — protector, pleaser, controller, isolator?
7. Which emotions have I judged or avoided because I believed they made me weak?

WEEK TWO — HEALING THE INNER STORY

Focus: origins, beliefs, narratives

8. What core belief do I carry about myself when I'm in pain?
9. Where did I learn it? Who modeled it?

10. What emotion did I suppress in order to be accepted, loved, or safe?
11. What unmet need hides beneath anger, jealousy, silence, or withdrawal?
12. What do I fear others would see if I stopped performing strength?
13. What does my shadow want me to finally acknowledge?
14. If I could rewrite the belief that hurts me most, what truth would I replace it with?

WEEK THREE — SELF-COMPASSION AND RELEASE

Focus: forgiveness, tenderness, self-reclamation

15. Which part of me deserves compassion instead of judgment?
16. What boundaries did I learn to survive that no longer serve me?
17. How can I show emotional safety to myself this week?
18. Where has guilt or shame kept me small?
19. What emotional or relational habit is ready to soften?
20. What would I tell my younger self now that I couldn't have known then?
21. What is the most honest apology I owe myself?

WEEK FOUR — INTEGRATION AND REBIRTH

Focus: empowerment, expansion, authenticity

22. What part of me is ready to come out of hiding?
23. Where do I feel more honest, grounded, and present than I did before?
24. What emotional reaction has softened, and what does that tell me about my healing?
25. How does my body feel when I tell myself the truth instead of the protective story?

26. What new boundaries, behaviors, or actions align with my healed self?
27. Where am I beginning to choose authenticity over approval?
28. When do I feel most aligned, authentic, and whole?
29. What parts of myself am I finally ready to integrate?
30. What does wholeness feel like — in my body, mind, emotions, and energy?

B. Post-Session Reflection Sheets

Use these after Reiki sessions, meditations, emotional triggers, journaling breakthroughs, or therapy conversations.

They help track:

- patterns
- insights
- emotional responses
- somatic shifts

Copy freely into a notebook or print multiple pages.

POST-SESSION REFLECTION SHEET

Date:
Time:
Session Type:
(☐ Self-Reiki ☐ Meditation ☐ Journal Work ☐ Session with Practitioner)

---

1. What emotion(s) surfaced most strongly?

(list or describe)
→ ____

2. Did any memories, images, or symbolic impressions appear?

→ ____

3. Where did I feel the emotion in my body?

☐ Chest
☐ Stomach/Solar Plexus
☐ Throat
☐ Head
☐ Hands
☐ Pelvis
☐ Legs/Feet
☐ Other: ____________________

Describe the sensation
→ ____________________________________

4. What belief arose during the session?

(e.g., "I'm unlovable," "I must not be weak," "I need to be perfect")
→ ____________________________________

5. If that belief belonged to a younger version of me, who was it?

Age, memory, or inner archetype
→ ____________________________________

6. How did Reiki shift the emotional field?

☐ Soften tension
☐ Released old emotion
☐ Brought clarity
☐ Opened compassion
☐ Calmed nervous system

☐ Revealed truth
☐ Other: ____________________________

Notes:
→ ____

7. What insight, lesson, or realization emerged?

→ ____

8. What gentle action or boundary feels right after this session?

→ ____

9. What do I need most from myself right now?

(compassion, rest, reassurance, silence, grounding)
→ ____

C. Emotional Trigger Tracker

This helps map patterns over time without self-blame.

Use daily or weekly.
You will begin to see:

- the core wound behind the reaction
- common triggers
- emotional progression
- reductions in intensity
- spiritual maturity

EMOTIONAL TRIGGER TRACKER

Date:
Time:
Triggering Event:
(brief description)
→ ____

Primary Emotion Felt:

☐ Anger
☐ Fear
☐ Shame
☐ Grief
☐ Jealousy
☐ Insecurity
☐ Disappointment
☐ Other: ___________

Intensity (0-10):

→ ________

Where I Felt It in My Body:

☐ Chest
☐ Stomach
☐ Throat
☐ Shoulders
☐ Jaw
☐ Head
☐ Pelvis
☐ Other: __________

Immediate Reaction / Impulse:

(freeze, withdraw, self-attack, numb, project, shut down)
→ ______________________________________

What Deeper Fear or Belief Was Activated?

→ ______________________________________

Shadow Archetype Noticed:

☐ The Victim
☐ The Saboteur
☐ The Inner Critic
☐ The Addict
☐ The Pleaser
☐ The Controller
☐ The Perfectionist
☐ Other: ___________

Did Reiki Shift Anything?

☐ Calmed the emotion
☐ Revealed deeper truth

☐ Helped me stay present
☐ Softened intensity
☐ Released old pain
☐ Opened compassion
☐ No change this time

Notes:
→ ____

How Did I Respond Instead of React?
→ ____

New Self-Affirmation I Choose Now:
→ ____

✦ CLOSING WORDS FOR THE JOURNAL SECTION

Shadow work is not about diagnosing yourself or proving progress.

It is about:

- witnessing patterns with honesty
- offering compassion to emotional truth
- recognizing subtle evolution
- anchoring wisdom into daily life

Every insight you write is integration in motion.
Every tracked trigger weakens old survival reflexes.
Every moment of self-reflection proves you are no longer abandoning yourself.

The shadow does not dissolve through force.
It softens in environments where truth is welcome.

And your journal becomes the proof:
You showed up.
You listened.
You stayed.
You healed.

Just for today, I will let go of worry and trust the flow of life.

Closing: The Return to Wholeness

If you have reached these final pages, it means you have walked bravely through the quiet corridors of your own being.
You have listened to the parts of yourself that once lived in hiding.
You have offered compassion to wounds that once felt too heavy to name.
You have stood before your shadow — not as an enemy, but as an equal.

This is not small work.
It is sacred work.

Reiki has illuminated the inner pathways, softened the closed doors, and reminded you that healing never asks you to erase who you have been — only to bring all that you are back into belonging.

As the journey of this book draws to its close, your journey of integration continues.

Shadow is not a phase or a problem.
It is the history of your sensitivity, the intelligence of your survival, and the voice of your most unguarded truth.
It carries the wisdom of every moment you endured, every boundary you learned to build, every fear you internalized, and every hope you hid to stay safe.

When you meet your shadow with tenderness, something remarkable happens:

It stops needing to protest.
It stops needing to protect.
It begins to trust you again.

The parts of you that once clenched in fear begin to breathe.
The emotions that once rushed like storms now flow like rivers.
The memories that once haunted you return as teachers.
And the space within you softens into coherence — where every fragment returns to the whole.

This is the heart of Reiki:
not fixing the self,
but remembering the truth beneath every scar.

You are not defined by your pain, your mistakes, your reactions, or your past.
You are the one who survived.
You are the one who chose to feel.
You are the one who came here seeking healing instead of silence.

That choice is evidence of your evolution.

Let these final truths settle deeply:

You are not unlovable — you were misunderstood by earlier versions of yourself.
You are not broken — you are unfolding.
You are not late — you are right on time.
Everything within you deserves a place at the table of your becoming.

The shadow taught you strength.
Reiki taught you compassion.

And together, they led you here — to the quiet knowing that wholeness is not perfection, but unity.

Keep this work alive by living in relationship with your inner world:

- Speak gently to yourself.
- Honor your limits.
- Validate your emotions.
- Let your truth matter.
- Trust your intuition.
- Return to Reiki when you shake.
- Place hands to heart when old wounds rise.

And when you find yourself at a new edge — unsure, triggered, grieving, or afraid — remember the words that shadow healing has whispered again and again:

"I stay with myself."

That is integration.
That is freedom.
That is love in its purest form.

Thank you for walking this path with courage.
Thank you for listening to the parts of you that once trembled in silence.
Thank you for choosing presence over avoidance, tenderness over denial, and truth over performance.

May you continue to meet your shadow with reverence.
May Reiki remain your light, your anchor, and your reminder.
May every part of you find its way home.

Wholeness was never lost.
It was only waiting for you to see it.

You are already enough.
You are already whole.
You are already healed.

And now —

you remember.

Closing Reflections: The Light You Carry Forward

If you are reading these final pages, it means you did something courageous:

You turned toward your inner shadows
instead of running from them.

That alone is healing.

Shadow work is not a destination, nor a single revelation.
It is a long remembering — a process of returning to yourself one layer, one truth, one breath at a time.

Reiki walks with you through that remembering.

This path was never about becoming perfect, purified, or spiritually flawless.
It has always been about becoming whole:

- lifting shame instead of burying it
- recognizing pain instead of numbing it
- listening to emotion instead of judging it
- embracing the parts of you that once felt unworthy, unlovable, or unseen

You have learned that darkness is not the enemy.
It is unintegrated intelligence — emotional history, ancestral echoes, nervous system protection, and spiritual potential, waiting for the warmth of your awareness.

Reiki does not erase suffering.
It brings light into the places we once feared to look.
In that light, the shadow becomes a teacher rather than a threat.

Through the meditations, techniques, rituals, symbols, and reflections in this book, you have been invited into sacred self-witnessing — a reclamation not just of your energy, but of your truth.

Carry forward what you've discovered:

- Allow emotion rather than resist it
- Speak gently to the parts that still feel tender
- Use Reiki as a bridge when inner storms rise
- Trust your intuition when deeper layers surface
- Honor every chapter of your story — even the chapters that still ache

And above all:

Meet your humanity with compassion.

Your inner light does not shine *in spite* of the darkness.
It shines more fully because you dared to walk into it.

Should new triggers surface
Should old patterns return
Should deeper layers of shadow call your name

Remember this:

You are more equipped now than ever before.
You know how to breathe
how to witness
how to offer Reiki to the wound instead of abandoning it.

You know how to listen.

Your shadow will evolve as you do.
Not as a lifetime of pain — but as a lifelong companion in growth.

Let every moment of self-awareness become an act of liberation.
Let every energetic shift become an act of grace.

Reiki is always within you — flowing through your hands, your intuition, and your capacity to love yourself honestly.

This journey does not end here.

It continues in the spaces where you choose truth over suppression, presence over numbness, curiosity over judgment, and compassion over fear.

When the next door within you opens, let Reiki walk with you again.

You are the light.
You are the healer.
You are the one you have been waiting for.

With reverence and belief in your wholeness,
Dr. Constance Santego
Grand Reiki Master

Glossary

Abandonment Wound

An emotional imprint formed from experiences (real or perceived) of being rejected, dismissed, or unsupported. Often results in fear of vulnerability, perfectionism, or self-silencing. Shadow work helps reveal and heal these origins.

Affirmation

A conscious statement used to counter internalized beliefs rooted in fear, shame, or self-rejection. When paired with Reiki, affirmations can help reinforce emotional safety and spiritual remembrance.

Aura

The energetic field that surrounds and interpenetrates the physical body. Shadow imprints, emotional memory, and defense patterns can present within the aura. Reiki supports clarity, flow, and balance.

Blockage (Energetic)

An interruption in emotional, mental, or spiritual energy flow, often rooted in unresolved pain, suppressed emotions, or trapped beliefs. Reiki encourages softening, release, and movement.

Chakras

Seven primary energy centers in the body, each associated with specific mental, emotional, physical, and spiritual themes. Chakra imbalance can reflect shadow patterns, trauma memories, or survival conditioning.

Compassion (Self-Compassion)

A gentle emotional posture toward oneself, especially toward inner wounds or difficult traits. Essential for shadow integration and nervous system safety.

Cord (Energetic)

A symbol or visualization representing emotional attachment, often formed through relationships, vows, or unresolved experiences. Reiki-based cord-release rituals support emotional freedom without erasing memory or meaning.

Dai Ko Myo

A Reiki Master symbol associated with spiritual remembrance, deep emotional integration, and illumination of inner truth. Used to soften shame, support soul-level healing, and restore coherence.

Emotional Trigger

A sudden emotional activation rooted in past experience, stored trauma, or internalized beliefs. Triggers are invitations to examine wounds that still need compassion. Reiki helps regulate the nervous system so triggers can be processed safely.

Energetic Imprint

The subtle emotional residue of past experiences, stored within the body, chakras, or aura. Imprints can shape beliefs, patterns, and reactions until consciously healed.

Energy Integration

The process of reconciling fragmented parts of the psyche, dissolving internal conflict, and restoring emotional coherence. Achieved through presence, shadow work, and Reiki.

Fight/Flight/Freeze/Fawn

Common nervous system responses to perceived threat:

- **Fight:** defensive emotion or aggression
- **Flight:** withdrawal, avoidance
- **Freeze:** emotional shutdown
- **Fawn:** people-pleasing for safety
  Shadow work brings awareness to these patterns so they can be replaced with conscious choices.

Hand Placements

Traditional Reiki practice of placing hands over chakras or body areas to invite healing flow. Used to calm triggers, release stored emotion, and bring shadow aspects into safety.

Higher Self

The intuitive aspect of consciousness connected to spiritual truth, compassion, and clarity. Reiki helps strengthen connection to this inner guidance.

Hon Sha Ze Sho Nen

A Reiki symbol used for distance healing, timeline support, ancestral patterns, inner child work, and emotional healing across past experiences.

Inner Child

The psychological and energetic imprint of earlier developmental stages, often carrying unmet needs, suppressed emotions, and survival beliefs. Reiki provides a safe bridge for listening, comforting, and integrating this aspect.

Integration

The gentle process of bringing hidden, suppressed, or rejected parts of oneself back into belonging. The goal of shadow work is not perfection, but wholeness.

Karmic Pattern

Emotional, relational, or behavioral cycles that repeat due to unresolved pain or unconscious belief. Reiki and shadow work help dissolve the emotional charge that fuels repetition.

Meditation (Reiki Meditation)

A state of inward awareness where breath, attention, and Reiki flow help soften defense patterns, reveal inner truth, and support emotional healing.

Nervous System Regulation

The process of restoring internal safety, calm, and coherence after activation or emotional overwhelm. Reiki naturally supports this through touch, presence, and breath.

Projection

A psychological defense where suppressed emotions or internal wounds are perceived as coming from others. Shadow work brings ownership, compassion, and clarity.

Reiki

A Japanese healing art based on channeling universal life force energy through intention, presence, and gentle hands-on technique. Used in this book as a framework for emotional integration and shadow work.

Reiki Attunement

A ceremonial initiation in which a Reiki Master empowers the student's connection to Reiki. Required for lineage-based training. Shadow work is safe to practice without attunement, but Reiki techniques in this book should be used respectfully.

Resistance

Emotional or mental tension that arises when the psyche feels unsafe to reveal inner truth. Reiki helps soften resistance by creating safety, presence, and compassion.

Sacral Chakra

Energy center associated with emotional truth, vulnerability, intimacy, and creative expression. Often holds suppressed feelings and self-rejection wounds.

Sei He Ki

A Reiki symbol used for emotional balancing, trauma release, and energetic harmony between the heart and mind. Core tool in shadow processing.

Self-Sabotage

Behaviors driven by fear, shame, or trauma memory that unconsciously prevent success, love, growth, or fulfillment. Viewed in shadow work not as failure, but as emotional protection asking for compassion.

Shadow

The unconscious part of the psyche that carries suppressed emotions, stored memories, survival strategies, and rejected traits. Shadow work honors these parts with compassion rather than judgment.

Shadow Archetypes

Inner patterns that emerge under emotional threat or psychological stress, e.g.:

- The Victim
- The Saboteur
- The Inner Critic
- The Addict
- The Controller
- The Pleaser
  They are not flaws — but survival strategies needing presence and understanding.

Solar Plexus Chakra

Energy center of identity, confidence, boundaries, and self-trust. A core site of shame, guilt, and inner rejection. Often activated during shadow healing.

Trauma Memory

Emotion or sensory imprint held in the body and subconscious, often without full conscious recall. Reiki creates safety so these impressions can surface gently without retraumatization.

Trigger Point Release

Using Reiki to dissolve emotional tension and energetic constriction within the body. Not physical manipulation — rather energetic softening.

Wholeness

The state of inner coherence where shadow and light are no longer fragmented. Healing does not erase pain — it transforms the relationship to the parts that carry it.

Witnessing

A position of compassionate observation, free from judgment or pressure. One of the most essential healing principles in shadow integration.

(ray)

Universal Life Energy
Spiritual Consciousness
All-Knowing

KI *(kee)*

Breath
Life Force
Vital Radiant Energy

Chokurei (Show Ku Ray)

Used for Physical Clearing.

Forward 7 is used for general or whole body, backward 7 is used for specific or small areas

Sei He Ki (Say Hey Key)

Used for Emotional Clearing and Mental Clearing

Hon Sha Ze Sho Nen, which is specifically associated with distant healing.

Bibliography

Reiki & Shadow Work: Healing the Dark Side of the Soul

Note: Classical origins of Reiki trace back primarily through oral lineage, practitioner transmission, and translated historical records. Shadow psychology is rooted in Jungian theory, with additional expansion through modern trauma and somatic research.

Primary Sources on Shadow Work, Depth Psychology & Archetypes

Jung, Carl Gustav. *Aion: Researches into the Phenomenology of the Self.* Princeton University Press, 1979.
— Foundational text establishing the structure of the psyche, the Shadow, and integration.

Jung, Carl Gustav. *The Archetypes and the Collective Unconscious.* Princeton University Press, 1981.
— Core source on inner archetypes, projection, symbolic interpretation, and transformation.

Ford, Debbie. *The Dark Side of the Light Chasers.* Riverhead Books, 1998.
— A modern interpretation of shadow integration as self-acceptance and emotional healing.

Johnson, Robert A. *Owning Your Own Shadow: Understanding the Dark Side of the Psyche.* HarperOne, 1991.

— A clear psychological mapping of the shadow, repression, and wholeness.

Zweig, Connie, and Jeremiah Abrams (Editors). *Meeting the Shadow: The Hidden Power of the Dark Side of Human Nature.* TarcherPerigee, 1991.
— A seminal anthology that collects perspectives on shadow dynamics from multiple scholars.

Inner Child, Trauma, and Emotional Integration

Bradshaw, John. *Homecoming: Reclaiming and Healing Your Inner Child.* Bantam Books, 1992.
— Explores emotional wounding and internal fragmentation caused by childhood conditioning.

Maté, Gabor. *The Myth of Normal: Trauma, Illness & Healing in a Toxic Culture.* Penguin Random House, 2022.
— Insights into how emotional suppression impacts wellbeing and how true healing integrates the past.

Levine, Peter A. *Waking the Tiger: Healing Trauma.* North Atlantic Books, 1997.
— Introduces somatic awareness, nervous-system regulation, and trauma imprinting.

Energy Healing, Reiki Lineage & Spiritual Integration

Petter, Frank Arjava. *Reiki Fire: New Information about the Origins of the Reiki Healing System.* Lotus Press, 1997.
— Explores the known teachings and history of Mikao Usui and Reiki's transmission.

Rand, William Lee. *Reiki: The Healing Touch.* Vision Publications, 1991.

— A reference manual on the foundational principles, symbols, hand positions, and applications of Reiki.

Usui, Mikao, and Frank Arjava Petter (Translator). *The Original Reiki Handbook of Dr. Mikao Usui.* Lotus Press, 1999.
— One of the closest available written teachings attributed to Usui's early healing methods.

Wauters, Ambika. *Chakras and Their Archetypes.* Crossing Press, 1988.
— Insightful work linking chakra function with psychological archetypes and personal evolution.

Spirituality, Consciousness, and Energetic Psychology

Kornfield, Jack. *A Path with Heart: A Guide Through the Perils and Promises of Spiritual Life.* Bantam, 1993.
— Gentle spiritual insight on compassion, inner struggle, and heart-centered awakening.

Moore, Thomas. *Care of the Soul: A Guide for Cultivating Depth and Sacredness in Everyday Life.* Harper Perennial, 1992.
— Philosophical and mystical perspectives on the inner landscapes of emotional life.

Tolle, Eckhart. *The Power of Now.* New World Library, 1997.
— Introduces presence and conscious awareness as keys to inner transformation and healing.

Modern Research on Emotion, Nervous System, and Self-Compassion

Neff, Kristin. *Self-Compassion: The Proven Power of Being Kind to Yourself.* HarperCollins, 2011.
— Foundational text on self-acceptance and reshaping inner emotional response.

Siegel, Daniel J. *The Developing Mind: How Relationships and the Brain Interact to Shape Who We Are.* Guilford Press, 1999.
— Integrates neuroscience, behavior, and emotional imprinting.

Somatic Practices, Breath, and Embodiment

Roth, Gabrielle. *Maps to Ecstasy: The Healing Power of Movement.* New World Library, 1989.
— Explores movement, emotional release, and embodiment as pathways to psyche-integration.

Van der Kolk, Bessel. *The Body Keeps the Score: Brain, Mind, and Body in the Healing of Trauma.* Penguin Books, 2015.
— Modern multidisciplinary work on trauma memory, body response, and integrative healing approaches.

Supplementary Sources & Philosophical Anchors

Campbell, Joseph. *The Hero with a Thousand Faces.* Princeton University Press, 2004.
— Useful lens for understanding the "descent," challenge, and rebirth inherent in shadow work.

Moore, Robert L. and Gillette, Douglas. *King, Warrior, Magician, Lover: Rediscovering the Archetypes of the Mature Masculine.* HarperOne, 1990.

— Archetypal mapping valuable for shadow reclamation in identity and power.

Message From The Author

Writing this book has been a journey through my own shadows — an honest exploration of the parts of myself I once resisted, judged, misunderstood, or tried to outrun. Shadow work is not a concept I studied from a distance. It is a landscape I walked through with trembling hands, closed doors, and moments of profound awakening.

For many years, I believed that healing meant transcending pain — rising above the past, silencing emotion, and "fixing what was wrong." Reiki taught me otherwise.

True healing is not escape.
It is embodiment.

It is remembrance.
It is forgiveness.
It is integration.

The shadow is not proof of our brokenness.
It is proof that we survived.

Within every wound is a fragment of self that once protected us the only way it knew how. And within every fragment is an invitation:

Come home. We are ready now.

Reiki entered my life as a gentle light — one that allowed me to see my own inner darkness not as an enemy, but as a teacher. Through its quiet intelligence, I discovered that shame softens in compassion. Fear dissolves in presence. And self-rejection melts in the warmth of unconditional awareness.

I wrote this book for the person who feels like they are carrying more than they can name.
For the one who senses there are unanswered questions beneath their reactions.
For the healer who gives so much and struggles to offer the same tenderness inward.

If that is you, I want you to know this:

You are not alone in your shadows.
You are not "behind."
You are not too sensitive, too emotional, too flawed, or too complicated.

You are becoming.

Every time you choose to face an inner truth, soften instead of shut down, breathe instead of deny, you are healing the unseen stories that echo through your body, your lineage, and your spirit.

Reiki brings grace to that journey.
It teaches us to sit with ourselves the way Spirit sits with us — patiently, lovingly, and without judgment.

If this book has offered you even one moment of clarity, compassion, courage, or emotional release, then its purpose has been fulfilled.

May your shadows become honored teachers.
May your inner child feel safe to rest.
May your heart remember its original innocence.
And may your spirit walk forward in the wholeness that has always been yours.

With love, reverence, and faith in your light,

Dr. Constance Santego
Grand Reiki Master / Elemental Healing Educator

About The Author

Dr. Constance Santego, DNM, Ph.D.
Grand Reiki Master • Natural Medicine Doctor • Bestselling Author & Educator

Dream BIGGER!

Dr. Constance Santego has devoted more than two decades to the study and practice of holistic healing, energy medicine, and spiritual transformation. A Natural Medicine Doctor and Grand Reiki Master, she has trained thousands of students in Reiki, integrative therapies, intuitive development, and the energetic principles of mind–body healing.

Her work blends classical Reiki lineage, Jungian psychological concepts, bioenergetics, and modern trauma-aware understanding. Through her teaching, writing, and practitioner training programs, Dr. Santego is known for bringing depth, clarity, and compassion to the inner healing journey — guiding others to awaken their own intuitive wisdom and spiritual sovereignty.

She is the author of over seventy published books, including the *Reiki Wisdom* series, *Secrets of a Healer*, and numerous works on energy medicine, consciousness, and spiritual gifts. Her teachings are rooted in the belief that healing is not about erasing wounds but integrating them — transforming shadow into insight and pain into power.

As a mentor and healer, she has supported students around the world in emotional release, karmic clearing, intuitive awakening, and return to wholeness. She continues to teach advanced Reiki training, practitioner certification programs, and spiritual development courses both in person and through her online learning platform.

When she is not writing or teaching, Dr. Santego enjoys the natural beauty of British Columbia, where she lives with her husband. Her mission remains clear: to help others experience the profound transformation that occurs when Reiki, compassion, and honest self-awareness meet.

ALSO AVAILABLE

Play the game *Ikona* – Discover Your Inner Genie

For additional information on

Constance Santego's

wide range of Motivational Products, Coaching Sessions,
Spiritual Retreats,
Live Events and Educational Programs

Go to

www.ConstanceSantego.ca

Follow on Instagram - Constance_Santego and
Facebook - constancesantegoo

Subscribe and receive Free Information and Meditations on my
YouTube Channel - Constance Santego

Companion Books

More is taught about Energy healing, Chakras, and Reiki in my book,

"Secrets of a Healer – Magic of Reiki (Vol X)

Trade paperback ISBN: 978-1-7772220-0-0
eBook ISBN 978-1-7772220-1-7

SECRETS OF A HEALER
VOL. XI
THE REIKI MASTER'S MANUAL

Trade paperback ISBN: 978-1-990062-34-6
eBook ISBN 978-1-990062-35-3

Angelic Lifestyle A Vibrant Lifestyle from a Grand Reiki Master

Trade paperback ISBN: 978-0-9952112-7-8

Angelic Lifestyle 42-Day Energy Cleanse

Trade paperback ISBN: 978-1-7770818-3-6
eBook ISBN 978-1-7770818-4-3

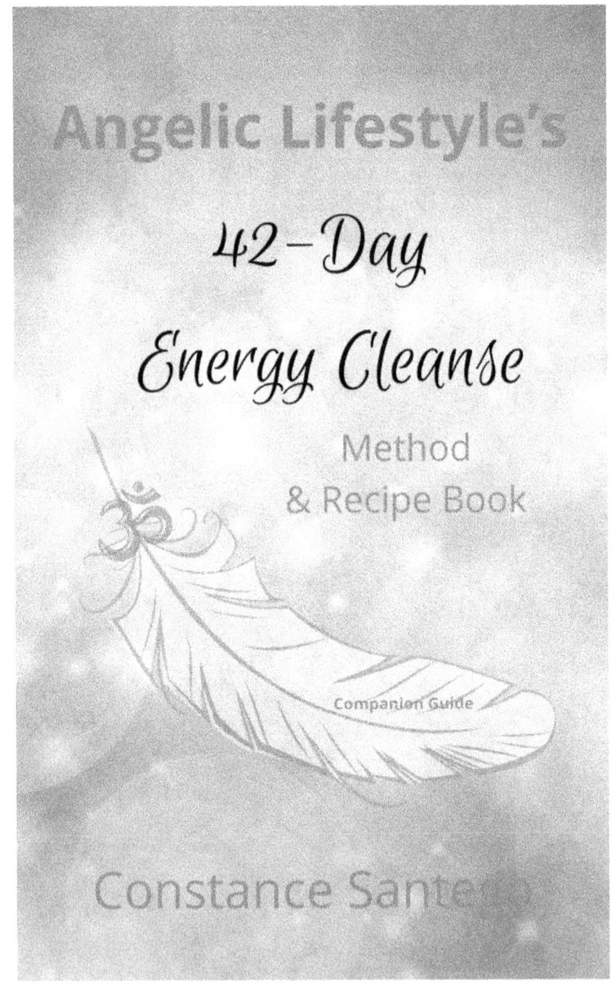

Just for today, I will let go of worry and trust the flow of life.

Reiki and the Power of The Joint Points

VOL. I OF THE REIKI WISDOM SERIES

Beyond the Symbols — The Path to True Mastery

Trade paperback ISBN: 978-1-990062-57-5
eBook ISBN 978-1-990062-58-2

from my "Novel" Series,
"The Nine Spiritual Gifts Granted By Spirit"
Vol IV in the series, ***"Miracles of a Soul"***

Soft Cover ISBN: 978-1-990062-12-4
eBook ISBN: 978-1-990062-13-1

Zen Coloring VOL II: Reiki Energy Journal

Therapeutic Art for Mind, Body, and Spirit

Soft Cover ISBN: 979-8324392697

Just for today, I will let go of worry and trust the flow of life.

Just for today, I will let go of worry and trust the flow of life.

www.ingramcontent.com/pod-product-compliance
Lightning Source LLC
Chambersburg PA
CBHW071710120626
46550CB00001B/173
* 9 7 8 1 9 9 7 9 0 7 1 6 9 *